D0472001

Node: Up and Running

Tom Hughes-Croucher and Mike Wilson

O'REILLY®

Beijing · Cambridge · Farnham · Köln · Sebastopol · Tokyo

Node: Up and Running

by Tom Hughes-Croucher and Mike Wilson

Published by O'Reilly Media, Inc., 1005 Gravenstein Highway North, Sebastopol, CA 95472.

O'Reilly books may be purchased for educational, business, or sales promotional use. Online editions are also available for most titles (*http://my.safaribooksonline.com*). For more information, contact our corporate/institutional sales department: (800) 998-9938 or *corporate@oreilly.com*.

Editors: Andy Oram and Simon St.Laurent		**Indexer:** Lucie Haskins	
Production Editor: Kristen Borg		**Cover Designer:** Karen Montgomery	
Copyeditor: Genevieve d'Entremont		**Interior Designer:** David Futato	
Proofreader: Rachel Monaghan		**Illustrators:** Robert Romano and Rebecca Demarest	

May 2012:   First Edition.

Revision History for the First Edition:
    2012-04-20   First release
See *http://oreilly.com/catalog/errata.csp?isbn=9781449398583* for release details.

ISBN: 978-1-449-39858-3

[LSI]

1334948772

Table of Contents

Part II. Deep Dive and API Reference

Foreword by Ryan Dahl

In 2008 I was searching for a new programming platform for making websites. This was more than wanting a new language; indeed, the details of the language mattered very little to me. Rather, I was concerned about the ability to program advanced push features into the website like I had seen in Gmail—the ability for the server to push data to the user instead of having to constantly poll. The existing platforms were tightly coupled to the idea of the server as something that receives a request and issues a response sequentially. To push events to the browser, the platform needed to be able to constantly handle a number of open and mostly idle connections.

I knew how to make this work at the system call layer, in C. If I used only nonblocking sockets, the overhead per connection was very small. In small tests, I could demonstrate a server that could handle thousands of idle connections or pretty massive throughput. I knew that this was the optimal way for a user-space Unix server to be implemented. However, I didn't want to work in C; I wanted the beautiful fluidity of a dynamic language. Although it was possible to issue the exact system calls I wanted in every programming language, it was very ugly and was always the "alternative" method of socket programming. My theory was that nonblocking sockets were not actually difficult at all, as long as everything was nonblocking.

Google announced Chrome and its new JavaScript engine V8 in late 2008. A faster JavaScript engine made for a faster Web—and V8 made the Web *a lot* faster. Suddenly there was this idea of a JavaScript arms race between Google, Apple, Mozilla, and Microsoft. This, combined with Doug Crockford's book *JavaScript: The Good Parts* (O'Reilly), shifted JavaScript from the language everyone despised to an important language.

I had an idea: nonblocking sockets in JavaScript! Because JavaScript has no existing socket libraries, I could be the first to introduce this new and hopefully better interface. Just take V8 and glue it to my nonblocking C code, and I should be done. I quit my contracting job and began working on this idea full time. Once I made the very first version available, I immediately had users who reported bugs; I started fixing those bugs, and then three years passed.

It turns out that JavaScript jibes extremely well with nonblocking sockets. This was not clear from the start. The closures made everything possible. People were able to build very complex nonblocking servers in just a couple of lines of JavaScript. My initial fear that the system would be unusably niche was quickly alleviated as hackers from all over the world began to build libraries for it. The single event loop and pure non-blocking interface allowed libraries to add more and more complexity without introducing expensive threads.

In Node, users find a system that scales well by default. Because of the choices made in the core system, nothing in the system is allowed to do anything too terrible (such as block the current thread), and thus performance never degrades horribly. It is an order of magnitude better than the traditional blocking approach, where "better" is defined as the amount of traffic it can handle.

These days, Node is being used by a large number of startups and established companies around the world, from Voxer and Uber to Walmart and Microsoft. It's safe to say that billions of requests are passing through Node every day. As more and more people come to the project, the available third-party modules and extensions grow and increase in quality. Although I was once reserved about recommending it for mission-critical applications, I now heartily recommend Node for even the most demanding server systems.

This book gracefully takes the reader through a discussion of and guided exercises for Node and many third-party modules. By learning the material covered here, you go from basic familiarity with JavaScript to building complex, interactive websites. If you've used other server-side web frameworks in the past, you'll be shocked at how easy it is to build a server in Node.

—Ryan Dahl, creator of Node.js

Foreword by Brendan Eich

In April 1995 I joined Netscape in order to "add Scheme to the browser." That recruiting bait from a month or two earlier immediately morphed into "do a scripting language that looks like Java." Worse, because the negotiation to put Java in Netscape was underway, some at Netscape doubted that a "second language" was necessary. Others wanted to build something like PHP, an HTML templating language for a planned server-side offering called LiveWire.

So in 10 days in May 1995, I prototyped "Mocha," the code name Marc Andreessen had chosen. Marc, Rick Schell (vice president of engineering at Netscape), and Bill Joy of Sun were the upper-management sponsors who supported my work against doubts about a "second language" after Java. (This is ironic since Java has all but disappeared in browsers, while JavaScript is dominant on the client side.)

To overcome all doubts, I needed a demo in 10 days. I worked day and night, and consequently made a few language-design mistakes (some recapitulating bad design paths in the evolution of LISP), but I met the deadline and did the demo.

People were amazed that I'd created a language compiler and runtime in less than two weeks, but I'd had a lot of practice over the decade since switching from a physics major in my third year to math/computer science. I had always loved formal language and automata theory. I'd built my own parsers and parser generators for fun. At Silicon Graphics, I built network-monitoring tools that included packet-header matching and protocol description languages and compilers. I was a huge fan of C and Unix. So knocking out "Mocha" was really a matter of sustained application and concentration.

Sometime in the fall of 1995, Netscape marketing renamed Mocha "LiveScript," to match the LiveWire server-side product name. Finally, in early December 1995, Netscape and Sun concluded a trademark license, signed by "Bill Joy, Founder" on behalf of Sun, and LiveScript was renamed JavaScript (JS).

Because of the LiveWire server plans, in the first 10 days I implemented a bytecode compiler and interpreter as well as a decompiler and runtime (the built-in JS objects and functions we know today: Object, Array, Function, etc.). For small client-side scripts, bytecode was overkill, but the LiveWire product included the feature of saving compiled bytecode for faster server-app startup.

Of course, Netscape's server-side JavaScript offering failed along with most of the rest of Netscape's business, as Microsoft tied Internet Explorer (IE) into Windows and entered the server markets into which Netscape was trying to diversify from its browser market, where commercial users who had once bought browser licenses no longer paid since IE was being bundled with Windows for free.

So in spite of LiveWire's failure, even in 1995 we could see the appeal of end-to-end JavaScript programming. Users saw it too, but this history is known only to a relative few today. And LiveWire made a fatal error that Node.js avoided: it embraced blocking input/output and a process-mob model on the server side...so it did not scale well.

Fast forward to the 2009's JSConf EU, where Ryan presented Node.js. I was gratified to learn of Node and to see how well it realized the end-to-end JavaScript vision, especially how it wisely built in nonblocking I/O from the roots up. Ryan and core folks have done a great job keeping the core small. Isaac and all the module owners have built an excellent module system to relieve pressure on the core, so it doesn't grow too large. And the Node community that has evolved around the code is excellent, too.

The result is a really productive, fun system for building servers, to complement the increasingly productive, fun JavaScript client side and to facilitate code reuse and co-evolution. Without Node, JavaScript would be still associated with its birthplace, the overconstrained client side of the Web, with the much-maligned Document Object Model and other historical accidents looming too large. Node helps JavaScript by freeing it from its limiting client-side patrimony.

This book nicely conveys the spirit of Node and the knowledge of how to use it well to build interactive web apps and sites. Node is a blast, and *Node: Up and Running* is a fitting guide for it. Enjoy!

—Brendan Eich, creator of JavaScript

Preface

Introduction

Node.js is quickly becoming one of the most influential technologies in the Web development community. This book aims to give programmers the information they need to effectively learn how to get started with Node.

This book expects you to have some understanding of JavaScript and programming in general, but we take the time to introduce you to the concepts that are important in event-driven programming on the server, rather than just focusing on the APIs that Node provides.

By reading this book you'll learn not just about Node, the platform, but also about some of the most important modules for Node that will let you quickly and effectively build highly scalable websites and services.

Conventions Used in This Book

The following typographical conventions are used in this book:

Italic
> Indicates new terms, URLs, email addresses, filenames, and file extensions.

`Constant width`
> Used for program listings, as well as within paragraphs to refer to program elements such as variable or function names, databases, data types, environment variables, statements, and keywords.

`Constant width bold`
> Shows commands or other text that should be typed literally by the user.

`Constant width italic`
> Shows text that should be replaced with user-supplied values or by values determined by context.

This icon signifies a tip, suggestion, or general note.

This icon indicates a warning or caution.

Using Code Examples

This book is here to help you get your job done. In general, you may use the code in this book in your programs and documentation. You do not need to contact us for permission unless you're reproducing a significant portion of the code. For example, writing a program that uses several chunks of code from this book does not require permission. Selling or distributing a CD-ROM of examples from O'Reilly books does require permission. Answering a question by citing this book and quoting example code does not require permission. Incorporating a significant amount of example code from this book into your product's documentation does require permission.

We appreciate, but do not require, attribution. An attribution usually includes the title, author, publisher, and ISBN. For example: "*Node: Up and Running* by Tom Hughes-Croucher and Mike Wilson (O'Reilly). Copyright 2012 Tom Hughes-Croucher and Mike Wilson, 978-1-449-39858-3."

If you feel your use of code examples falls outside fair use or the permission given above, feel free to contact us at *permissions@oreilly.com*.

Safari® Books Online

 Safari Books Online (*www.safaribooksonline.com*) is an on-demand digital library that delivers expert content in both book and video form from the world's leading authors in technology and business.

Technology professionals, software developers, web designers, and business and creative professionals use Safari Books Online as their primary resource for research, problem solving, learning, and certification training.

Safari Books Online offers a range of product mixes and pricing programs for organizations, government agencies, and individuals. Subscribers have access to thousands of books, training videos, and prepublication manuscripts in one fully searchable database from publishers like O'Reilly Media, Prentice Hall Professional, Addison-Wesley Professional, Microsoft Press, Sams, Que, Peachpit Press, Focal Press, Cisco Press, John Wiley & Sons, Syngress, Morgan Kaufmann, IBM Redbooks, Packt, Adobe Press, FT Press, Apress, Manning, New Riders, McGraw-Hill, Jones & Bartlett, Course

Technology, and dozens more. For more information about Safari Books Online, please visit us online.

How to Contact Us

Please address comments and questions concerning this book to the publisher:

O'Reilly Media, Inc.
1005 Gravenstein Highway North
Sebastopol, CA 95472
800-998-9938 (in the United States or Canada)
707-829-0515 (international or local)
707-829-0104 (fax)

We have a web page for this book, where we list errata, examples, and any additional information. You can access this page at:

http://oreil.ly/node_upandrunning

To comment or ask technical questions about this book, send email to:

bookquestions@oreilly.com

For more information about our books, courses, conferences, and news, see our website at *http://www.oreilly.com*.

Find us on Facebook: *http://facebook.com/oreilly*

Follow us on Twitter: *http://twitter.com/oreillymedia*

Watch us on YouTube: *http://www.youtube.com/oreillymedia*

Acknowledgments

Tom's Thanks

To my editors. Simon, it has been a long project, but you've been with me week after week. Andy, your eye for detail never fails to impress.

To Carlos. Your drive and talent make you the writer I would like to be. You are an inspiration.

To Nicole and Sean, for keeping me on track.

To Ryan and Isaac, who have put up with my endless stupid questions with the quiet patience of someone teaching a child.

To Rosemarie. Without you, I would never be where I am today.

To my friends, who have listened to my bitching (especially Yta, Emily, Eric, Gris, Sarah, Allan, Harold and Daniella, and Hipster Ariel). To the countless people who have given me encouragement, suggestions, and feedback. I couldn't have done it without you.

To the readers of this tome, thank you for trusting me with your learning.

## PART I

Up and Running

## CHAPTER 1

A Very Brief Introduction to Node.js

Node.js is many things, but mostly it's a way of running JavaScript outside the web browser. This book will cover why that's important and the benefits that Node.js provides. This introduction attempts to sum up that explanation in a few paragraphs, rather than a few hundred pages.

Many people use the JavaScript programming language extensively for programming the interfaces of websites. Node.js allows this popular programming language to be applied in many more contexts, in particular on web servers. There are several notable features about Node.js that make it worthy of interest.

Node is a wrapper around the high-performance V8 JavaScript runtime from the Google Chrome browser. Node tunes V8 to work better in contexts other than the browser, mostly by providing additional APIs that are optimized for specific use cases. For example, in a server context, manipulation of binary data is often necessary. This is poorly supported by the JavaScript language and, as a result, V8. Node's `Buffer` class provides easy manipulation of binary data. Thus, Node doesn't just provide direct access to the V8 JavaScript runtime. It also makes JavaScript more useful for the contexts in which people use Node.

V8 itself uses some of the newest techniques in compiler technology. This often allows code written in a high-level language such as JavaScript to perform similarly to code written in a lower-level language, such as C, with a fraction of the development cost. This focus on performance is a key aspect of Node.

JavaScript is an event-driven language, and Node uses this to its advantage to produce highly scalable servers. Using an architecture called an *event loop*, Node makes programming highly scalable servers both easy and safe. There are various strategies that are used to make servers performant. Node has chosen an architecture that performs very well but also reduces the complexity for the application developer. This is an extremely important feature. Programming concurrency is hard and fraught with danger. Node sidesteps this challenge while still offering impressive performance. As always, any approach still has trade-offs, and these are discussed in detail later in the book.

To support the event-loop approach, Node supplies a set of "nonblocking" libraries. In essence, these are interfaces to things such as the filesystem or databases, which operate in an event-driven way. When you make a request to the filesystem, rather than requiring Node to wait for the hard drive to spin up and retrieve the file, the nonblocking interface simply notifies Node when it has access, in the same way that web browsers notify your code about an `onclick` event. This model simplifies access to slow resources in a scalable way that is intuitive to JavaScript programmers and easy to learn for everyone else.

Although not unique to Node, supporting JavaScript on the server is also a powerful feature. Whether we like it or not, the browser environment gives us little choice of programming languages. Certainly, JavaScript is the only choice if we would like our code to work in any reasonable percentage of browsers. To achieve any aspirations of sharing code between the server and the browser, we must use JavaScript. Due to the increasing complexity of client applications that we are building in the browser using JavaScript (such as Gmail), the more code we can share between the browser and the server, the more we can reduce the cost of creating rich web applications. Because we must rely on JavaScript in the browser, having a server-side environment that uses JavaScript opens the door to code sharing in a way that is not possible with other server-side languages, such as PHP, Java, Ruby, or Python. Although there are other platforms that support programming web servers with JavaScript, Node is quickly becoming the dominant platform in the space.

Aside from what you can build *with* Node, one extremely pleasing aspect is how much you can build *for* Node. Node is extremely extensible, with a large volume of community modules that have been built in the relatively short time since the project's release. Many of these are drivers to connect with databases or other software, but many are also useful software applications in their own right.

The last reason to celebrate Node, but certainly not the least important, is its community. The Node project is still very young, and yet rarely have we seen such fervor around a project. Both novices and experts have coalesced around the project to use and contribute to Node, making it both a pleasure to explore and a supportive place to share and get advice.

Installing Node.js

Installing Node.js is extremely simple. Node runs on Windows, Linux, Mac, and other POSIX OSes (such as Solaris and BSD). Node.js is available from two primary locations: the project's website (*http://nodejs.org*) or the GitHub repository (*http://github.com/joyent/node*). You're probably better off with the Node website because it contains the stable releases. The latest cutting-edge features are hosted on GitHub for the core development team and anyone else who wants a copy. Although these features are new and often intriguing, they are also less reliable than those in a stable release.

Let's get started by installing Node.js. The first thing to do is download Node.js from the website, so let's go there and find the latest release. From the Node home page, find the download link. The current release at the time of print is 0.6.13, which is a stable release. The Node website provides installers for Windows and Mac as well as the stable source code. If you are on Linux, you can either do a source install or use your usual package manager (apt-get, yum, etc.).

 Node.js version numbers follow the C convention of *major.minor* *.patch*. Stable versions of Node.js have an even minor version number, and development versions have an odd minor version number. It's unclear when Node will become version 1, but it's a fair assumption that it will only be when the Windows and Unix combined release is considered mature.

If you used an installer, you can skip to "First Steps in Code" on page 7. Otherwise (i.e., if you are doing a source install), once you have the code, you'll need to unpack it. The tar command does this using the flags xzf. The x stands for extract (rather than compress), z tells tar to also decompress using the GZIP algorithm, and f indicates we are unpacking the filename given as the final argument (see Example 1-1).

Example 1-1. Unpacking the code

```
enki:Downloads $ tar xzf node-v0.6.6.tar.gz
enki:Downloads $ cd node-v0.6.6
enki:node-v0.6.6 $ ls
AUTHORS       Makefile       common.gypi    doc       test
BSDmakefile   Makefile-gyp   configure      lib       tools
ChangeLog     README.md      configure-gyp  node.gyp  vcbuild.bat
LICENSE       benchmark      deps           src       wscript
enki:node-v0.6.6 $
```

The next step is to configure the code for your system. Node.js uses the configure/make system for its installation. The configure script looks at your system and finds the paths Node needs to use for the dependencies it needs. Node generally has very few dependencies. The installer requires Python 2.4 or greater, and if you wish to use TLS or cryptology (such as SHA1), Node needs the OpenSSL development libraries. Running configure will let you know whether any of these dependencies are missing (see Example 1-2).

Example 1-2. Configuring the Node install

```
enki:node-v0.6.6 $ ./configure
Checking for program g++ or c++       : /usr/bin/g++
Checking for program cpp              : /usr/bin/cpp
Checking for program ar               : /usr/bin/ar
Checking for program ranlib           : /usr/bin/ranlib
Checking for g++                      : ok
Checking for program gcc or cc        : /usr/bin/gcc
Checking for gcc                      : ok
```

```
Checking for library dl               : yes
Checking for openssl                  : not found
Checking for function SSL_library_init : yes
Checking for header openssl/crypto.h  : yes
Checking for library util             : yes
Checking for library rt               : not found
Checking for fdatasync(2) with c++    : no
'configure' finished successfully (0.991s)
enki:node-v0.6.6 $
```

The next installation step is to make the project (Example 1-3). This compiles Node and builds the binary version that you will use into a build subdirectory of the source directory we've been using. Node numbers each of the build steps it needs to complete so you can follow the progress it makes during the compile.

Example 1-3. Compiling Node with the make command

```
enki:node-v0.6.6 $ make
Waf: Entering directory `/Users/sh1mmer/Downloads/node-v0.6.6/out'
DEST_OS: darwin
DEST_CPU: x64
Parallel Jobs: 1
Product type: program
[ 1/35] copy: src/node_config.h.in -> out/Release/src/node_config.h
[ 2/35] cc: deps/http_parser/http_parser.c -> out/Release/deps/http_parser/http_parser_3.o
/usr/bin/gcc -rdynamic -pthread -arch x86_64 -g -O3 -DHAVE_OPENSSL=1 -D_LARGEFILE_SOURCE ...
[ 3/35] src/node_natives.h: src/node.js lib/dgram.js lib/console.js lib/buffer.js ...
[ 4/35] uv: deps/uv/include/uv.h -> out/Release/deps/uv/uv.a

...

f: Leaving directory `/Users/sh1mmer/Downloads/node-v0.6.6/out'
'build' finished successfully (2m53.573s)
-rwxr-xr-x  1 sh1mmer  staff   6.8M Jan  3 21:56 out/Release/node
enki:node-v0.6.6 $
```

The final step is to use make to install Node. First, Example 1-4 shows how to install Node globally for the whole system. This requires you to have either access to the root user or sudo privileges that let you act as root.

Example 1-4. Installing Node for the whole system

```
enki:node-v0.6.6 $ sudo make install
Password:
Waf: Entering directory `/Users/sh1mmer/Downloads/node-v0.6.6/out'
DEST_OS: darwin
DEST_CPU: x64
Parallel Jobs: 1
Product type: program
* installing deps/uv/include/ares.h as /usr/local/include/node/ares.h
* installing deps/uv/include/ares_version.h as /usr/local/include/node/ares_version.h
* installing deps/uv/include/uv.h as /usr/local/include/node/uv.h

...
```

```
* installing out/Release/src/node_config.h as /usr/local/include/node/node_config.h
Waf: Leaving directory `/Users/sh1mmer/Downloads/node-v0.6.6/out'
'install' finished successfully (0.915s)
enki:node-v0.6.6 $
```

If you want to install only for the local user and avoid using the sudo command, you need to run the configure script with the --prefix argument to tell Node to install somewhere other than the default (Example 1-5).

Example 1-5. Installing Node for a local user

```
enki:node-v0.6.6 $ mkdir ~/local
enki:node-v0.6.6 $ ./configure --prefix=~/local
Checking for program g++ or c++          : /usr/bin/g++
Checking for program cpp                 : /usr/bin/cpp

...

'configure' finished successfully (0.501s)
enki:node-v0.6.6 $ make && make install
Waf: Entering directory `/Users/sh1mmer/Downloads/node-v0.6.6/out'
DEST_OS: darwin
DEST_CPU: x64

...

* installing out/Release/node as /Users/sh1mmer/local/bin/node
* installing out/Release/src/node_config.h as /Users/sh1mmer/local/include/node/...
Waf: Leaving directory `/Users/sh1mmer/Downloads/node-v0.6.6/out'
'install' finished successfully (0.747s)
enki:node-v0.6.6 $
```

First Steps in Code

This section will take you through a basic Node program before we move on to more in-depth programs.

Node REPL

One of the things that's often hard to understand about Node.js is that, in addition to being a server, it's also a runtime environment in the same way that Perl, Python, and Ruby are. So, even though we often refer to Node.js as "server-side JavaScript," that doesn't really accurately describe what Node.js does. One of the best ways to come to grips with Node.js is to use Node REPL ("Read-Evaluate-Print-Loop"), an interactive Node.js programming environment. It's great for testing out and learning about Node.js. You can try out any of the snippets in this book using Node REPL. In addition, because Node is a wrapper around V8, Node REPL is an ideal place to easily try out JavaScript. However, when you want to run a Node program, you can use your favorite text editor, save it in a file, and simply run node filename.js. REPL is a great learning and exploration tool, but we don't use it for production code.

Let's launch Node REPL and try out a few bits of JavaScript to warm up (Example 1-6). Open up a console on your system. I'm using a Mac with a custom command prompt, so your system might look a little different, but the commands should be the same.

Example 1-6. Starting Node REPL and trying some JavaScript

```
$Enki:~ $ node
> 3 > 2 > 1
false
> true == 1
true
> true === 1
false
```

 The first line, which evaluates to false, is from *http://wtfjs.com*, a collection of weird and amusing things about JavaScript.

Having a live programming environment is a really great learning tool, but you should know a few helpful features of Node REPL to make the most of it. It offers meta-commands, which all start with a period (.). Thus, .help shows the help menu, .clear clears the current context, and .exit quits Node REPL (see Example 1-7). The most useful command is .clear, which wipes out any variables or closures you have in memory without the need to restart REPL.

Example 1-7. Using the metafeatures in Node REPL

```
> console.log('Hello World');
Hello World
> .help
.clear    Break, and also clear the local context.
.exit     Exit the prompt
.help     Show repl options
> .clear
Clearing context...
> .exit
Enki:~ $
```

When using REPL, simply typing the name of a variable will enumerate it in the shell. Node tries to do this intelligently so a complex object won't just be represented as a simple Object, but through a description that reflects what's in the object (Example 1-8). The main exception to this involves functions. It's not that REPL doesn't have a way to enumerate functions; it's that functions have the tendency to be very large. If REPL enumerated functions, a lot of output could scroll by.

Example 1-8. Setting and enumerating objects with REPL

```
Enki:~ $ node
> myObj = {};
{}
> myObj.list = ["a", "b", "c"];
[ 'a', 'b', 'c' ]
> myObj.doThat = function(first, second, third) { console.log(first); };
[Function]
> myObj
{ list: [ 'a', 'b', 'c' ]
, doThat: [Function]
}
>
```

A First Server

REPL gives us a great tool for learning and experimentation, but the main application of Node.js is as a server. One of the specific design goals of Node.js is to provide a highly scalable server environment. This is an area where Node differs from V8, which was described at the beginning of this chapter. Although the V8 runtime is used in Node.js to interpret the JavaScript, Node.js also uses a number of highly optimized libraries to make the server efficient. In particular, the HTTP module was written from scratch in C to provide a very fast nonblocking implementation of HTTP. Let's take a look at the canonical Node "Hello World" example using an HTTP server (Example 1-9).

Example 1-9. A Hello World Node.js web server

```
var http = require('http');
http.createServer(function (req, res) {
    res.writeHead(200, {'Content-Type': 'text/plain'});
    res.end('Hello World\n');
}).listen(8124, "127.0.0.1");
console.log('Server running at http://127.0.0.1:8124/');
```

The first thing that this code does is use `require` to include the HTTP library into the program. This concept is used in many languages, but Node uses the CommonJS module format, which we'll talk about more in Chapter 8. The main thing to know at this point is that the functionality in the HTTP library is now assigned to the `http` object.

Next, we need an HTTP server. Unlike some languages, such as PHP, that run inside a server such as Apache, Node itself acts as the web server. However, that also means we have to create it. The next line calls a factory method from the HTTP module that creates new HTTP servers. The new HTTP server isn't assigned to a variable; it's simply going to be an anonymous object in the global scope. Instead, we use chaining to initialize the server and tell it to listen on port 8124.

When calling `createServer`, we passed an anonymous function as an argument. This function is attached to the new server's event listener for the `request` event. Events are central to both JavaScript and Node. In this case, whenever there is a new request to the web server, it will call the method we've passed to deal with the request. We call these kinds of methods *callbacks* because whenever an event happens, we "call back" all the methods listening for that event.

Perhaps a good analogy would be ordering a book from a bookshop. When your book is in stock, they *call back* to let you know you can come and collect it. This specific callback takes the arguments req for the request object and res for the response object.

Inside the function we created for the callback, we call a couple of methods on the res object. These calls modify the response. Example 1-9 doesn't use the request, but typically you would use both the request and response objects.

The first thing we *must* do is set the HTTP response header. We can't send any actual response to the client without it. The res.writeHead method does this. We set the value to 200 (for the HTTP status code "200 OK") and pass a list of HTTP headers. In this case, the only header we specify is Content-type.

After we've written the HTTP header to the client, we can write the HTTP body. In this case, we use a single method to both write the body and close the connection. The end method closes the HTTP connection, but since we also passed it a string, it will send that to the client before it closes the connection.

Finally, the last line of our example uses the console.log. This simply prints information to stdout, much like the browser counterpart supported by Firebug and Web Inspector.

Let's run this with Node.js on the console and see what we get (Example 1-10).

Example 1-10. Running the Hello World example

```
Enki:~ $ node
> var http = require('http');
> http.createServer(function (req, res) {
...     res.writeHead(200, {'Content-Type': 'text/plain'});
...     res.end('Hello World\n');
...     }).listen(8124, "127.0.0.1");
> console.log('Server running at http://127.0.0.1:8124/');
Server running at http://127.0.0.1:8124/
node>
```

Here we start a Node REPL and type in the code from the sample (we'll forgive you for pasting it from the website). Node REPL accepts the code, using ... to indicate that you haven't completed the statement and should continue entering it. When we run the console.log line, Node REPL prints out Server running at http://127.0.0.1:8124/. Now we are ready to call our Hello World example in a web browser (Figure 1-1).

It works! Although this isn't exactly a stunning demo, it is notable that we got Hello World working in six lines of code. Not that we would recommend that style of coding, but we are starting to get somewhere. In the next chapter, we'll look at a lot more code, but first let's think about why Node is how it is.

Figure 1-1. Viewing the Hello World web server from a browser

Why Node?

In writing this book, we've been acutely aware of how new Node.js is. Many platforms take years to find adoption, and yet there's a level of excitement around Node.js that we've never seen before in such a young platform. We hope that by looking at the reasons other people are getting so excited about Node.js, you will find features that also resonate with you. By looking at Node.js's strengths, we can find the places where it is most applicable. This section looks at the factors that have come together to create a space for Node.js and discusses the reasons why it's become so popular in such a short time.

High-Performance Web Servers

When we first started writing web applications more than 10 years ago, the Web was much smaller. Sure, we had the dot-com bubble, but the sheer volume of people on the Internet was considerably lower, and the sites we made were much less ambitious. Fast-forward to today, and we have the advent of Web 2.0 and widely available Internet connections on cell phones. So much more is expected of us as developers. Not only are the features we need to deliver more complex, more interactive, and more real, but there are also many more people using them more often and from more devices than ever before. This is a pretty steep challenge. While hardware continues to improve, we also need to make improvements to our software development practices to support such demands. If we kept just buying hardware to support ever-increasing features or users, it wouldn't be very cost-effective.

Node is an attempt to solve this problem by introducing the architecture called *event-driven computing* to the programming space for web servers. As it turns out, Node isn't the first platform to do this, but it is by far the most successful, and we would argue that it is the easiest to use. We are going to talk about event-driven programming in a lot more detail later in this book, but let's go through a quick intro here. Imagine you connect to a web server to get a web page. The time to reach that web server is probably 100ms or so over a reasonable DSL connection. When you connect to a typical web server, it creates a new instance of a program on the server that represents your request. That program runs from the top to the bottom (following all of the function calls) to provide your web page. This means that the server has to allocate a fixed amount of memory to that request until it is totally finished, including the 100ms+ to send the data back to you. Node doesn't work that way. Instead, Node keeps all users in a single program. Whenever Node has to do something slow, like wait for a confirmation that you got your data (so it can mark your request as finished), it simply moves on to another user. We're glossing over the details a bit, but this means Node is much more efficient with memory than traditional servers and can keep providing a very fast response time with lots and lots of concurrent users. This is a huge win. This approach is one of the main reasons people like Node.

Professionalism in JavaScript

Another reason people like Node is JavaScript. JavaScript was created by Brendan Eich in 1995 to be a simple scripting language for use in web pages on the Netscape browser platform. Surprisingly, almost since its inception JavaScript has been used in non-browser settings. Some of the early Netscape server products supported JavaScript (known then as LiveScript) as a server-side scripting language. Although server-side JavaScript didn't really catch on then, that certainly wasn't true for the exploding browser market. On the Web, JavaScript competed with Microsoft's VBScript to provide programming functionality in web pages. It's hard to say why JavaScript won, but perhaps Microsoft allowing JavaScript in Internet Explorer did it,[1] or perhaps it was the JavaScript language itself, but win it did. This meant by the early 2000s, JavaScript had emerged as *the* web language—not just the first choice, but the *only* choice for programming with HTML in browsers.

What does this have to do with Node.js? Well, the important thing to remember is that when the AJAX revolution happened and the Web became big business (think Yahoo!, Amazon, Google, etc.), the only choice for the "J" in AJAX was JavaScript. There simply wasn't an alternative. As a result, a whole industry needed an awful lot of JavaScript programmers, and really good ones at that, rather fast. The emergence of the Web as a serious platform and JavaScript as its programming language meant that we, as JavaScript programmers, needed to shape up. We can equate the change in JavaScript as the second or third programming language of a programmer to the change in perception of its importance. We started to get emerging experts who led the charge in making JavaScript respectable.

Arguably at the head of this movement was Douglas Crockford. His popular articles and videos on JavaScript have helped many programmers discover that inside this much-maligned language there is a lot of beauty. Most programmers working with JavaScript spent the majority of their time working with the browser implementation

---

1. Internet Explorer doesn't actually support JavaScript or ECMAScript; it supports a language variety called JScript. In recent years, JScript has fully supported the ECMAScript 3 standard and has some ECMAScript 5 support. However, JScript also implements proprietary extensions in the same way that Mozilla JavaScript does and has features that ECMAScript does not.

---

of the W3C DOM API for manipulating HTML or XML documents. Unfortunately, the DOM is probably not the prettiest API ever conceived, but worse, its various implementations in the browsers are inconsistent and incomplete. No wonder that for a decade after its release JavaScript was not thought of as a "proper" language by so many programmers. More recently, Douglas's work on "the good parts" of JavaScript have helped create a movement of advocates of the language who recognize that it has a lot going for it, despite the warts.

In 2012, we now have a proliferation of JavaScript experts advocating well-written, performant, maintainable JavaScript code. People such as Douglas Crockford, Dion Almaer, Peter Paul Koch (PPK), John Resig, Alex Russell, Thomas Fuchs, and many more have provided research, advice, tools, and primarily libraries that have allowed thousands of professional JavaScript programmers worldwide to practice their trade with a spirit of excellence. Libraries such as jQuery, YUI, Dojo, Prototype, Mootools, Sencha, and many others are now used daily by thousands of people and deployed on millions of websites. It is in this environment—where JavaScript is not only accepted, but widely used and celebrated—that a platform larger than the Web makes sense. When so many programmers know JavaScript, its ubiquity is a distinct advantage.

When a roomful of web programmers is asked what languages they use, Java and PHP are very popular, Ruby is probably the next most popular these days (or at least closely tied with Python), and Perl still has a huge following. However, almost without exception, anyone who does any programming for the Web has programmed in JavaScript. Although backend languages are fractured in-browser, programming is united by the necessities of deployment. Various browsers and browser plug-ins allow the use of other languages, but they simply aren't universal enough for the Web. So here we are with a single, universal web language. How can we get it on the server?

Browser Wars 2.0

Fairly early in the days of the Web, we had the infamous *browser wars*. Internet Explorer and Netscape competed viciously on web features, adding various incompatible programmatic features to their own browser and not supporting the features in the other browser. For those of us who programmed for the Web, this was the cause of much anguish because it made web programming really tiresome. Internet Explorer more or less emerged as the winner of that round and became the dominant browser. Fast-forward a few years, and Internet Explorer has been languishing at version 6, and a new contender, Firefox, emerges from the remnants of Netscape. Firefox kicks off a resurgence in browsers, followed by WebKit (Safari) and then Chrome. Most interesting about this current trend is the resurgence of competition in the browser market.

Unlike the first iteration of the browser wars, today's browsers compete on two fronts: adhering to the standards that emerged after the previous browser war, and performance. As websites have become more complex, users want the fastest experience possible. This has meant that browsers not only need to support the web standards well, allowing developers to optimize, but also to do a little optimization of their own. With JavaScript as a core component of Web 2.0, AJAX websites have become part of the battleground.

Each browser has its own JavaScript runtime: Spider Monkey for Firefox, Squirrel Fish Extreme for Safari, Karakan for Opera, and finally V8 for Chrome. As these runtimes compete on performance, it creates an environment of innovation for JavaScript. And in order to differentiate their browsers, vendors are going to great lengths to make them as fast as possible.

## CHAPTER 2

Doing Interesting Things

The programming trends of the last few years have made it progressively easier to write more complex applications with ease. It's important that we don't lose that, but Node is specifically focused on solving the problem of building *network* applications—that is, applications that do a lot of input/output (I/O). Let's build a few I/O-type apps and see how easy it is to do this with Node in a way that really scales.

Building a Chat Server

In a world that's increasingly real-time, what is more real-time than chat? So where should we begin? Let's start with a TCP-based chat server we can connect to with Telnet. Not only is it a simple place to start, but it's also something we can write 100% in Node.

The first thing we need to do is include the TCP libraries from Node and create a new TCP server (see Example 2-1).

Example 2-1. Creating a new TCP server

```
var net = require('net')

var chatServer = net.createServer()

chatServer.on('connection', function(client) {
  client.write('Hi!\n');
  client.write('Bye!\n');

  client.end()
})

chatServer.listen(9000)
```

First, we include the net module. This contains all the TCP stuff for Node. From that, we can create a TCP server by calling the net.createServer() method. Now that we have a server, we want it to do stuff. So we add an event listener by using the on() method. Whenever the connection event happens, the event listener will call the function we gave it. A connection event happens when a new client connects to the server.

The connection event passes us a reference to the TCP socket for our new client when it calls our callback function. We named this reference client. By calling client.write(), we can send messages to the newly connected client. To start with, we just say "Hi!" and then "Bye!", and we call the client.end() method, which closes the connection. It's simple, but it's a starting point for our chat server. Finally, we need to call listen() so Node knows which port to listen on. Let's test it.

We can test our new server by connecting to it with the Telnet program, which is installed on most operating systems.[1] First, we need to start our server by calling node with the filename. Then we can connect by opening a Telnet connection to local host on port 9000, as we specified in our Node program. See Example 2-2.

Example 2-2. Connecting to a Node TCP server with Telnet

```
Console Window 1
----------------
Enki:~ $ node chat.js
Chat server started


Console Window 2
----------------
Last login: Tue Jun  7 20:35:14 on ttys000
Enki:~ $ telnet 127.0.0.1 9000
Trying 127.0.0.1...
Connected to localhost.
Escape character is '^]'.
Hi!
Bye!
Connection closed by foreign host.
Enki:~ $
```

So far we've made a server that clients can connect to, and we've sent them a message before kicking them out, but it's hardly a chat server. Let's add a few more things. First, we should make sure we can get messages from the clients, as shown in Example 2-3.

Example 2-3. Listening to each connection

```
var net = require('net')

var chatServer = net.createServer()
```

---

1. If you are on Windows, we recommend using the free Putty program as a Telnet client.

```
chatServer.on('connection', function(client) {
  client.write('Hi!\n');

  client.on('data', function(data) {
    console.log(data)
  })

})

chatServer.listen(9000)
```

Here we've added another event listener, and this time it's client.on(). Notice how we've added the event listener in the scope of the connection callback function. Doing this means we have access to the client that is passed to that event. The listener we've added is for an event called data. This is the event that is called each time client sends some data to the server. We've had to lose the client.end(), though. If we closed the connection to the client, how could we listen for new data? Now whenever we send data to the server, it will be outputted to the console. Let's try that in Example 2-4.

Example 2-4. Sending data to the server from Telnet

```
Console 1
-------------

Enki:~ $ node chat.js
Chat server started
<Buffer 48 65 6c 6c 6f 2c 20 79 6f 75 72 73 65 6c 66 0d 0a>

Console 2
------------
Enki:~ $ telnet 127.0.0.1 9000
Trying 127.0.0.1...
Connected to localhost.
Escape character is '^]'.
Hi!
Hello, yourself
```

What has happened here? We ran the server and connected to it with Telnet. The server said "Hi!" and we responded with "Hello, yourself". At this point, Node spat out a bunch of seeming gibberish in a data type you've never seen before. Because JavaScript doesn't have a good way to deal with binary data, Node added one. It's called Buffer, and it lets the server represent binary data. Node doesn't know what kind of data Telnet sent, so Node simply stores the data as binary until we ask for it in some other kind of encoding. The sequence of letters and numbers is actually bytes in hex (see "Buffers" on page 70 in Chapter 4 for more on this). Each byte represents one of the letters or characters in the string "Hello, yourself". We can use the toString() method to translate Buffer data into a regular string again if we want, or we can just pass it around as it is because TCP and Telnet understand the binary, too.

Now that we can get messages from each client, we should let them send each other messages. To do this, we need a way of letting them communicate with each other. It's great that we can call client.write(), but that works on only one client at a time. What we need is a way to reference other clients. We can do this by creating a list of clients that we want to write data to. Whenever we get a new client, we'll add it to our list and use the list to communicate between the clients (see Example 2-5).

Example 2-5. Communicating between clients

```
var net = require('net')

var chatServer = net.createServer(),
    clientList = []

chatServer.on('connection', function(client) {
  client.write('Hi!\n');

  clientList.push(client)

  client.on('data', function(data) {
    for(var i=0;i<clientList.length;i+=1) {
      //write this data to all clients
      clientList[i].write(data)
    }
  })

})

chatServer.listen(9000)
```

Now when we run it in Example 2-6, we can connect multiple clients to the server to see them sending messages to each other.

Example 2-6. Sending messages between clients

```
Console 1
------------

Enki:~ $ node chat.js


Console 2
------------

Enki:~ $ telnet 127.0.0.1 9000
Trying 127.0.0.1...
Connected to localhost.
Escape character is '^]'.
Hi!
Hello, yourself
Hello, yourself
```

```
Console 3
------------

Enki:~ $ telnet 127.0.0.1 9000
Trying 127.0.0.1...
Connected to localhost.
Escape character is '^]'.
Hi!
Hello, yourself
```

This time, the server isn't logging any messages it receives, and instead we loop through
the array and send them back to the clients. Notice that when the Telnet client in
terminal 2 sends a message, it gets sent to the Telnet client in terminal 3, but it also gets
sent back to Telnet in terminal 2 as well. This is because when we send the message,
we aren't checking who the sender was; we just send to our entire array of clients. It's
also not clear just by looking at Telnet which messages were things we sent and which
were things we received. We can improve on this. In Example 2-7, let's create a function
to send messages to all the clients, and use it to tidy up some of these issues.

Example 2-7. Improving the sending of messages

```
var net = require('net')

var chatServer = net.createServer(),
    clientList = []

chatServer.on('connection', function(client) {
  client.name = client.remoteAddress + ':' + client.remotePort
  client.write('Hi ' + client.name + '!\n');

  clientList.push(client)

  client.on('data', function(data) {
    broadcast(data, client)
  })

})

function broadcast(message, client) {
  for(var i=0;i<clientList.length;i+=1) {
    if(client !== clientList[i]) {
      clientList[i].write(client.name + " says " + message)
    }
  }
}

chatServer.listen(9000)
```

The first thing we've added to the connection event listener is a command to add a
name property to each client. Note how we are able to decorate the client object with
additional properties. This is because the closure binds each client object to a specific
request. The existing properties of the client are used to create the name, and the

client.remoteAddress is the IP address the client is connecting from. The client .remotePort is the TCP port that the client asked the server to send data back to. When multiple clients connect from the same IP, they will each have a unique remotePort. When we issue a greeting to the client, we can now do it using a unique name for that client.

We also extracted the client write loop from the data event listener. We now have a function called broadcast and, using it, we can send a message to all the connected clients. However, this time we pass the client that is sending the message (data) so we can exclude it from getting the message. We also include the sending client name (now that it has one) when sending the message to the other clients. This is a much better version of the server, as shown in Example 2-8.

Example 2-8. Running the improved chat server

```
Console 1
---------

Enki:~ $ node chat.js

Console 2
---------

Enki:~ $ telnet 127.0.0.1 9000
Trying 127.0.0.1...
Connected to localhost.
Escape character is '^]'.
Hi 127.0.0.1:56022!
Hello
127.0.0.1:56018 says Back atcha

Console 3
---------

Enki:~ $ telnet 127.0.0.1 9000
Trying 127.0.0.1...
Connected to localhost.
Escape character is '^]'.
Hi 127.0.0.1:56018!
127.0.0.1:56022 says Hello
Back atcha
```

This is a much friendlier and more useful service. It's still not perfect, but we are making progress. Note that the exact port numbers used in the names will almost certainly vary for you when you run this example. Different operating systems allow different port ranges, and the assignment will also depend on which ones you are already using, as well as a random factor. You may have already encountered this, but our server has a fatal flaw! If one of the clients disconnects, the server will fail horribly, as demonstrated in Example 2-9.

Example 2-9. Causing the server to fail by disconnecting a client

```
Console 1
----------

Enki:~ $ node book-chat.js  ❶

net.js:392 ❷
    throw new Error('Socket is not writable');
          ^
Error: Socket is not writable
    at Socket._writeOut (net.js:392:11)
    at Socket.write (net.js:378:17)
    at broadcast (/Users/sh1mmer/book-chat.js:21:21)
    at Socket.<anonymous> (/Users/sh1mmer/book-chat.js:13:5)
    at Socket.emit (events.js:64:17)
    at Socket._onReadable (net.js:679:14)
    at IOWatcher.onReadable [as callback] (net.js:177:10)
Enki:~ $

Console 2
---------

Enki:~ $ telnet 127.0.0.1 9000 ❸
Trying 127.0.0.1...
Connected to localhost.
Escape character is '^]'.
Hi 127.0.0.1:56910!
^]
telnet> quit ❹
Connection closed.
Enki:~ $

Console 3
---------

Enki:~ $ telnet 127.0.0.1 9000 ❺
Trying 127.0.0.1...
Connected to localhost.
Escape character is '^]'.
Hi 127.0.0.1:56911!
You still there? ❻
Connection closed by foreign host. ❼
Enki:~ $
```

We start the server as normal ❶ and connect some clients ❸❺, but when the client in Console 2 disconnects ❹, we have a bit of a problem. The next time we use broad cast(), in this case when Console 3 sends a message ❻, the server tries to write to a disconnected client ❷. When the client from Console 2 disconnected ❹, its socket stopped being writable or readable. When we try to call write() on a socket that is closed, we get an exception in the Node process. This also causes the disconnection of all the remaining clients ❼. Obviously, this is extremely brittle and not acceptable for a server.

We should fix this in two ways. First, we should make sure that when a client disconnects, we remove it from the clients array so it stops getting write() method calls. This
will also allow V8 to garbage-collect the socket object and reclaim that memory. Second, we should be a bit more defensive when we write to a socket. We want to make
sure that between the last time the socket was written and the current pass, nothing
has stopped us from being able to call write(). Happily, Node has easy ways to achieve
both of these things. The first is shown in Example 2-10.

Example 2-10. Making the chat server more robust

```
chatServer.on('connection', function(client) {
  client.name = client.remoteAddress + ':' + client.remotePort
  client.write('Hi ' + client.name + '!\n');

  clientList.push(client)

  client.on('data', function(data) {
    broadcast(data, client)
  })

  client.on('end', function() {
    clientList.splice(clientList.indexOf(client), 1)
  })
})
```

First, let's deal with those disconnecting clients. When a client disconnects, we want
to be able to remove it from the list of clients. This is easy to achieve with the end event.
When a socket disconnects, it fires the end event to indicate that it's about to close. We
can call Array.splice() when this happens to remove the client from the clientList
array. Using Array.indexOf(), we are able to find the position of this client. splice()
then removes from the array one item, which is the client. Now when the next
client uses the broadcast call, the disconnected client will no longer be in the list.

We can still be a bit more defensive, though, as demonstrated in Example 2-11.

Example 2-11. Checking the write status of sockets

```
function broadcast(message, client) {
  var cleanup = []
  for(var i=0;i<clientList.length;i+=1) {
    if(client !== clientList[i]) {

      if(clientList[i].writable) {
        clientList[i].write(client.name + " says " + message)
      } else {
        cleanup.push(clientList[i])
        clientList[i].destroy()
      }

    }
  }
}
```

```
//Remove dead Nodes out of write loop to avoid trashing loop index
for(i=0;i<cleanup.length;i+=1) {
    clientList.splice(clientList.indexOf(cleanup[i]), 1)
  }
}
```

By adding a check for the write status of the socket during the broadcast call, we can make sure that any sockets that are not available to be written don't cause an exception. Moreover, we can make sure that any sockets that can't be written to are closed (using `Socket.destroy()`) and then removed from the `clientList`. Note that we don't remove the sockets from the `clientList` while we are looping through it, because we don't want to cause side effects on the current loop we are in. Our server is now much more robust. There is one more thing we should do before we are really ready to deploy it: log the errors (Example 2-12).

Example 2-12. Logging errors

```
chatServer.on('connection', function(client) {
  client.name = client.remoteAddress + ':' + client.remotePort
  client.write('Hi ' + client.name + '!\n');
  console.log(client.name + ' joined')

  clientList.push(client)

  client.on('data', function(data) {
    broadcast(data, client)
  })

  client.on('end', function() {
    console.log(client.name + ' quit')
    clientList.splice(clientList.indexOf(client), 1)
  })

  client.on('error', function(e) {
    console.log(e)
  })
})
```

By adding a `console.log()` call to the `error` event for the `client` objects, we can ensure that any errors that occur to clients are logged, even as our previous code makes sure that clients throwing errors are not able to cause the server to abort with an exception.

Let's Build Twitter

The previous example shows how easy it is to write something extremely real-time with Node, but often you just want to write a web application. Let's try to create something similar to Twitter with Node so we can see what it's like to make a web application. The first thing we should do is install the Express module (Example 2-13). This web framework for Node makes it much easier to create web applications by adding support for common tasks, such as MVC, to the existing `http` server.

Example 2-13. Installing the Express module

```
Enki:~ $ npm install express
express@2.3.12 ./node_modules/express
├── mime@1.2.2
├── connect@1.5.1
└── qs@0.1.0
Enki:~ $
```

Installing Express is easy using the Node Package Manager (npm). Once we have the framework installed, we can make a basic web application (Example 2-14). This looks a lot like the application we built in Chapter 1.

 You can read more about npm in Chapters 6 and 7.

Example 2-14. A basic web server with Express

```
var express = require('express')

var app = express.createServer()

app.get('/', function(req, res) {
  res.send('Welcome to Node Twitter')
})

app.listen(8000)
```

This code looks pretty similar to the basic web server code from Chapter 1. Instead of including the http module, however, we include express. Express is actually getting http behind the scenes, but we don't have to get that ourselves, because Node will automatically resolve the dependencies. Like with http and net, we call create Server() to make a server and call listen() to make it listen to a specific port. Instead of attaching an event listener to the request event with Express, we can call methods matching the HTTP verbs. In this case, when we call get(), we can create a callback function that will match GET requests only to a URL that matches the first argument of the call. This has immediately added two things that the http server didn't have: the ability to filter based on HTTP verbs, and the ability to filter based on specific URLs.

When we get the callback, it looks a lot like the one from the http server—because it is. However, Express has added some extra methods. With the http server, we needed to create the HTTP headers and send them to the client before sending the body of the request. Express provides a convenience method on the res (http.response) object call named send(), and this method issues both the HTTP headers as well as a response.end() call. So far, we haven't done much more than the original Hello World server from Chapter 1. However, this server will respond only to a GET request to /

without throwing an error. This is in contrast to the previous example, which would respond to any request with any path.

Let's start adding some features to this server in order to provide some of the Twitter functionality (Example 2-15). At least to start with, we aren't going to worry about making it super-robust or scalable. We are going to make a few assumptions so you can see how to create applications.

Example 2-15. Adding a basic API

```
var express = require('express')

var app = express.createServer()
app.listen(8000)

var tweets = []

app.get('/', function(req, res) {
  res.send('Welcome to Node Twitter')
})

app.post('/send', express.bodyParser(), function(req, res) {
  if (req.body && req.body.tweet) {
    tweets.push(req.body.tweet)
    res.send({status:"ok", message:"Tweet received"})
  } else {
    //no tweet?
    res.send({status:"nok", message:"No tweet received"})
  }
})

app.get('/tweets', function(req,res) {
  res.send(tweets)
})
```

Building on the basic Express app, we've added a couple of functions to provide an extremely basic API. But first let's talk about another change we made. We moved the `app.listen()` call to the top of the file. It's important to understand why this doesn't cause a race condition for the functions that respond to requests. You might imagine that when we call `app.listen()`, any requests that happen between the `app.listen()` call and the time it takes to run those functions will be ignored. This is incorrect for two reasons. The first is that in JavaScript everything happens in an event loop. That means new events don't get called until we've finished evaluating the code of the existing loop pass. In this case, no `request` events will be called (and thus our `request`-based functions) until we've evaluated all the initialization code in the file. The other reason is that the `app.listen()` call is actually asynchronous because binding to a TCP port takes time. The addition of event listeners (via `app.get()` and `app.post()`), on the other hand, is synchronous.

To get some very basic tweeting action going, we've added a POST "route" for /send using the app.post() call. This call is a little bit different from the previous example. Obviously, it's an app.post() rather than an app.get() request. This simply means it accepts HTTP POST requests instead of HTTP GET requests. The significant difference is that we've passed an extra argument to the function. You don't need to do this on all app.post() calls, or any, in fact. The extra argument after the url is a *middleware*.

A middleware is a small piece of code that sits in between the original request event and the route we defined with app.post(). We use middleware to reuse code for common tasks such as authentication or logging. In this case the middleware's job is to stream the POST data from the client and then turn it into a JavaScript object that we can use. This middleware is one that is included in Express itself, called bodyParser. We simply include it by specifying it in the arguments we give to the app.post() route. Notice that we call express.bodyParser(). This function call actually returns another function. We use this standard style for middleware to allow you to pass configuration to the middleware if you want to.

If we didn't include the middleware, we would have to manually write code to accept the data event provided by the request (req) object. Only after we had streamed in all the POST data could we call the code in the app.post() route. Using the middleware not only helps with code reuse but also with clarity.

The express.bodyParser adds a property to req called req.body. This property (if it exists) contains an object representing the POST data. The express.bodyParser middleware will work only for POST requests with the content-type HTTP header of application/x-www-form-urlencoded or application/json. Both of these are easy to parse into key/value pairs as properties of the req.body object.

This means that in the app.post() route we made, the first thing we do is check whether express.bodyParser found any data. We can simply check to see whether req.body was created. If it was, we look for a property called req.body.tweet to represent the tweet. If we find a tweet, we stash it in a global array called tweets and send a JSON string back to the client noting success. If we couldn't find req.body or req.body.tweet, we send JSON back to the client, noting the failure. Notice how we didn't serialize the data in the res.send() calls. If we give res.send() an object, it automatically serializes it as JSON and sends the correct HTTP headers.

Finally, to make our basic API complete, we create an app.get() route that listens to /tweets. This route simply sends back JSON for the tweets array.

We can write a few tests for our simple API to make sure it's working (Example 2-16). This is a good habit to get into, even if you don't do full test-driven development (TDD).

Example 2-16. A test for the POST API

```
var http = require('http'),
    assert = require('assert')
```

```
var opts = {
  host: 'localhost',
  port: 8000,
  path: '/send',
  method: 'POST',
  headers: {'content-type':'application/x-www-form-urlencoded'}
}

var req = http.request(opts, function(res) {
  res.setEncoding('utf8')

  var data = ""
  res.on('data', function(d) {
    data += d
  })

  res.on('end', function() {
    assert.strictEqual(data, '{"status":"ok","message":"Tweet received"}')
  })
})

req.write('tweet=test')
req.end()
```

We need the http and assert[2] modules in order to send HTTP requests and then test the values returned. assert is a core module in Node that lets us test return values in various ways. When a value doesn't match the expected criteria, an exception is thrown. By making test scripts that check an expected behavior of our program, we can ensure that it is doing what it should be.

The http library doesn't just contain objects to serve HTTP; it also provides a client. In this test program, we use the http.request() factory method to create a new http.Request object. To create an http.Request, we need an *options object*. This is a configuration object we pass that has a list of properties defining the functionality we want the http.Request to exhibit. You'll see config objects used for constructing other Node objects. In this case, we include the hostname (which will be resolved by dns), the port, URL path, HTTP method, and some HTTP headers. Here the settings of the config object reflect what we used when creating our Express server.

The http.request() constructor takes two arguments: the first is the config object, and the second is a callback. The callback is attached to the response event for the http.Request. It's similar to an http.Server, except we have only one object in the response.

The first thing we do with the response is call setEncoding(). This allows us to define the encoding of all the received data. By setting this to utf8, we ensure that any data we receive will be treated as the right kind of string. Next, we define a variable, data, which we are going to use to stream all the responses from the server. In Express,

---

2. You can read more about assert in Chapter 5.

we can use `express.bodyDecoder` to catch all the data in a request and stream it, but we don't have the same luxury in the client, so we'll do it by hand. It's really easy. We simply attach a function to the `data` event on `response`. Whenever `data` happens, we append it to our `data` variable. We can listen for the `end` event of the `response` and then take further action on all of the data. The API is set up this way because there are many applications in which it is possible to stream data. In these cases, we can do all of the work in the `data` event listener rather than aggregating first.

When we get the `end` event on `response`, it's because we have all the data from the server. Now we can run our test on whatever the server sent. Our test in this case is to check whether the `data` variable has received what we expected from the server. If the server is acting correctly, it should send us back a piece of JSON. By using `assert.strict Equal`, we are checking that data matches the expected data using `===`. If it doesn't, an `assert` exception is thrown. We are using the `x-www-form-urlencoded` format because that's what a web page form would send.

Now that we've set up the `request` and the event handlers for it, we need to write some data to the server. Calling `write()` on `request` lets us send data (since this is a POST request). We send some test data to ensure that the server will respond correctly. Finally, we call `end()` to indicate that we are finished sending data with the `request` object.

When we call this script, it will access the server we set up (if it is running) and send a POST request. If it gets back the correct data, it will finish without output. If it can't connect to the server or if the server responds with the wrong output, it will throw an exception. The goal is to have a set of scripts we can run to check that the server is behaving correctly as we build it.

Now that we have an API, we can start adding a web interface so that people can use our app. Right now, it's basic, but the API allows people to send messages that everyone can receive. Let's make an interface to that.

Express supports an MVC (model, view, controller) approach oriented around the routing of requests. The routes act like controllers, providing a way to join the data model with a view. We've already used a route (`app.get('/', function)`). In the folder structure shown in Example 2-17, we can see where we host the different parts of the views. By convention, the *views* folder holds the view templates, and within it a *partials* folder contains the "partial views" (we'll discuss these more later). For applications that don't use a content delivery network (CDN), the *public* folder is used to store static files, such as CSS and JavaScript.

Example 2-17. The basic folder structure of an Express app

```
.
├── app.js
├── public
└── views
    └── partials
```

To start connecting our very simple model (`var tweets = []`) with a view, we need to create some views first. We are going to create some basic view files and put them in the *views* folder. Express offers a few different templating languages and is extensible to allow the addition of more. We are going to start with EJS.[3] EJS simply embeds JavaScript into the templates with a few simple tags to define how the JavaScript is interpreted. Let's take a look at an example of EJS, starting with the layout file in Example 2-18.

Example 2-18. EJS layout file

```
<!DOCTYPE html>
<html lang="en">
    <head>
      <meta charset="utf-8">
      <%- partial('partials/stylesheet', stylesheets) %>
      <title><%= title %></title>
    </head>
    <body>
        <h1><%= header %></h1>
        <%- body %>
    </body>
</html>
```

The layout file in Express defines a skeleton to use for your site. It's some basic view boilerplate you will use almost everywhere. In this case, we've used a very simple HTML5 page. It has a head with some stylesheet definitions and a body. The body consists of an `h1` header element and some content. Notice the `<%` tags. These are the places in which we are going to insert JavaScript variables. The JavaScript to be evaluated is between the `<%` and `%>` tags. The tags can also start with = or -, which we will discuss in more detail shortly. Mostly you'll just reference a piece of data. You can simply list the variable or reference you wish to include in the page. For example, `<h1><%= header %></h1>` includes the variable `header` into the `h1` element.

There are two special things used in this template. The first is the call to `partial()`. Partials are mini-templates for code that is expected to repeat again and again with different data. For example, you can imagine the comments on a blog post are the same snippet of HTML repeating many times, but with different pieces of information for each commenter and the comment she made. The actual HTML template doesn't change. Partials are a way to represent and store those small pieces of code that repeat often, independently of the pages that include them, to make it easy to update the code on all the pages at once. The other special thing in this layout template is the `body` variable. Because we use the layout template on all the pages on the site (unless we turn it off), we need some way to say where the specific template being rendered goes. Express provides the `body` variable for this task. This variable will contain the rendered contents of the specific template we load.

---

3. More of Express's view languages are covered in Chapter 7.

Let's make a render call from a route to see what that looks like before we explore the other templates we'll need (Example 2-19).

Example 2-19. Rendering the index template from the '/' route

```
app.get('/', function(req, res) {
  var title = 'Chirpie',
      header = 'Welcome to Chirpie'

  res.render('index', {
    locals: {
      'title': title,
      'header': header,
      'tweets': tweets,
      stylesheets: ['/public/style.css']
    }
  })
})
```

The route code looks like the other route code we've used. However, instead of calling `res.send()`, we use `res.render()` as the call to render a template. The first argument is the name of the specific template we want to render. Remember that whatever is in the index template will be rendered into the layout template where the body variable was. The second argument we pass to `res.render()` is a configuration object. In this case, we haven't done any configuration, except providing some local variables. The `locals` property of the config object contains the data used to render this template. We've passed in a title, a header, the array of tweets, and an array of stylesheets. All of these variables will be available to both the layout template and the index template.

We want to define an index template that is going to take the list of tweets and render them so that everyone can see the messages being posted (Example 2-20). We aren't going to do individual tweet streams just yet, but we can make a page in which everyone can see all the messages being posted and post their own messages using the API.

Example 2-20. An index template to show tweets and let people post new tweets

```
<form action="/send" method="POST">
  <input type="text" length="140" name="tweet">
  <input type="submit" value="Tweet">
</form>
<%- partial('partials/chirp', tweets) %>
```

This index template is really simple. We have a small form to provide an input method for new tweets. That's just regular HTML, but we can make it more AJAX-y later. We also have a partial for the tweets. Because they are all the same, we don't want to put in an ugly loop with some markup embedded in the index template. By using a partial, we can make one smaller template to represent tweets in those templates in which we want to include them. This keeps the code nice and DRY.[4] We can add more stuff later,

---

4. Don't repeat yourself.

but this gives us the basic functionality we need. We'll still need to define the partial templates we use in the layout template and the index template (Examples 2-21 and 2-22).

Example 2-21. A partial template for rendering chirps

```
<p><%= chirp %></p>
```

Example 2-22. A partial template for rendering stylesheets

```
<link rel="stylesheet" type="text/css" href="<%- stylesheet %>">
```

Both of these templates are really simple as well. They take some data and insert it into the markup. Because they get passed an array, they will repeat for each item in the array; however, neither of them is doing anything complex with the items of data. The variable each partial is using to access the array is the same as the name of the template. The template called `chirp` accesses its data in a variable of the same name. In this case, the data is simple strings, but if we passed in an array of objects, we could do `chirp` `.property` or `chirp['property']` to access the properties of the objects. Of course, you can also call methods, such as `chirp.method()`.

Now we have an application that allows us to post tweets. It's very basic, and there are some things that are pretty suboptimal. Let's correct a few of those things. The first obvious problem is that when we post a new tweet, it takes us to the "send JSON" endpoint. It's not bad that we are accessing `/send`, but rather that it treats all clients the same. The tweets are also coming out in chronological order and we haven't been saving a timestamp, so we don't know how fresh they are. We'll fix that too.

Fixing the `/send` endpoint is pretty simple. When HTTP clients send a request, they can specify the kind of response they want in order of preference. Typical browsers request `text/html` first and then various other formats. When performing API requests, however, the client can specify `application/json` in order to get the correct output. By checking for the `accept` HTTP header, we can make sure we send browsers back to the home page but simply return JSON to API clients.

The `accept` HTTP header might look like `text/html,application/xhtml+xml,applica tion/xml;q=0.9,*/*;q=0.8`. That header is from the Chrome browser, and it contains a number of MIME types separated by commas. First, we need a small function to figure out whether `text/html` is in the `accept` header (Example 2-23), and then we can use that to test the header and do some logic in the route.

Example 2-23. A small function to check for text/html in an accept header

```
function acceptsHtml(header) {
  var accepts = header.split(',')
  for(i=0;i<accepts.length;i+=0) {
    if (accepts[i] === 'text/html') { return true }
  }
```

```
    return false
}
```

This function splits the header across the commas. Then we iterate over that array and simply return true if any of them match text/html; otherwise, we'll return false if none of them matched. We can use this in our route function to check whether it is a request from a web browser or an API request (Example 2-24).

Example 2-24. Redirect web browsers from the /send endpoint

```
app.post('/send', express.bodyParser(), function(req, res) {
  if (req.body && req.body.tweet) {

    tweets.push(req.body.tweet)

    if(acceptsHtml(req.headers['accept'])) {
      res.redirect('/', 302)
    } else {
      res.send({status:"ok", message:"Tweet received"})
    }

  } else {
    //no tweet?
    res.send({status:"nok", message:"No tweet received"})
  }
})
```

Much of this code is the same as Example 2-10, but now we have a check for whether the accept header asks for text/html. If it does, we redirect back to / using the res .redirect command. We use a 302 status code because this isn't a permanent move. Instead, we want the browser to still go to /send each time before redirecting.

## CHAPTER 3

Building Robust Node Applications

To make the most of the server-side JavaScript environment, it's important to understand some core concepts behind the design choices that were made for Node.js and JavaScript in general. Understanding the decisions and trade-offs will make it easier for you to write great code and architect your systems. It will also help you explain to other people why Node.js is different from other systems they've used and where the performance gains come from. No engineer likes unknowns in her system. "Magic" is not an acceptable answer, so it helps to be able to explain why a particular architecture is beneficial and under what circumstances.

This chapter will cover the coding styles, design patterns, and production know-how you need to write good, robust Node code.

The Event Loop

A fundamental part of Node is the *event loop*, a concept underlying the behavior of JavaScript as well as most other interactive systems. In many languages, event models are bolted onto the side, but JavaScript events have always been a core part of the language. This is because JavaScript has always dealt with user interaction. Anyone who has used a modern web browser is accustomed to web pages that do things "onclick," "onmouseover," etc. These events are so common that we hardly think about them when writing web page interaction, but having this event support in the language is incredibly powerful. On the server, instead of the limited set of events based on the user-driven interaction with the web page's DOM, we have an infinite variety of events based on what's happening in the server software we use. For example, the HTTP server module provides an event called "request," emitted when a user sends the web server a request.

The event loop is the system that JavaScript uses to deal with these incoming requests from various parts of the system in a sane manner. There are a number of ways people deal with "real-time" or "parallel" issues in computing. Most of them are fairly complex and, frankly, make our brains hurt. JavaScript takes a simple approach that makes the process much more understandable, but it does introduce a few constraints. By having a grasp of how the event loop works, you'll be able to use it to its full advantage and avoid the pitfalls of this approach.

Node takes the approach that all I/O activities should be nonblocking (for reasons we'll explain more later). This means that HTTP requests, database queries, file I/O, and other things that require the program to wait do not halt execution until they return data. Instead, they run independently, and then emit an event when their data is available. This means that programming in Node.js has lots of callbacks dealing with all kinds of I/O. Callbacks often initiate other callbacks in a cascading fashion, which is very different from browser programming. There is still a certain amount of linear setup, but the bulk of the code involves dealing with callbacks.

Because of this somewhat unfamiliar programming style, we need to look for patterns to help us effectively program on the server. That starts with the event loop. We think that most people intuitively understand event-driven programming because it is like everyday life. Imagine you are cooking. You are chopping a bell pepper and a pot starts to boil over (Figure 3-1). You finish the slice you are working on, and then turn down the stove. Rather than trying to chop and turn down the stove at the same time, you achieve the same result in a much safer manner by rapidly switching contexts. Event-driven programming does the same thing. By allowing the programmer to write code that only ever works on one callback at a time, the program is both understandable and also able to quickly perform many tasks efficiently.

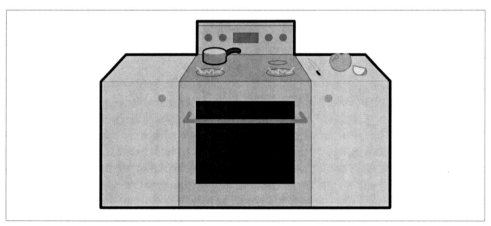

Figure 3-1. Event-driven people

In everyday life, we are used to having all sorts of internal callbacks for dealing with events, and yet, like JavaScript, we always do just one thing at once. Yes, yes, we can see that you are rubbing your tummy and patting your head at the same time—well done. But if you try to do any serious activities at the same time, it goes wrong pretty quickly. This is like JavaScript. It's great at letting events drive the action, but it's "single-threaded" so that only one thing happens at once.

This single-threaded concept is really important. One of the criticisms leveled at Node.js fairly often is its lack of "concurrency." That is, it doesn't use all of the CPUs on a machine to run the JavaScript. The problem with running code on multiple CPUs at once is that it requires coordination between multiple "threads" of execution. In order for multiple CPUs to effectively split up work, they would have to talk to each other about the current state of the program, what work they'd each done, etc. Although this is possible, it's a more complex model that requires more effort from both the programmer and the system. JavaScript's approach is simple: there is only one thing happening at once. Everything that Node does is nonblocking, so the time between an event being emitted and Node being able to act on that event is very short because it's not waiting on things such as disk I/O.

Another way to think about the event loop is to compare it to a postman (or mailman). To our event-loop postman, each letter is an event. He has a stack of events to deliver in order. For each letter (event) the postman gets, he walks to the route to deliver the letter (Figure 3-2). The route is the callback function assigned to that event (sometimes more than one). Critically, however, because our postman has only a single set of legs, he can walk only a single code path at a time.

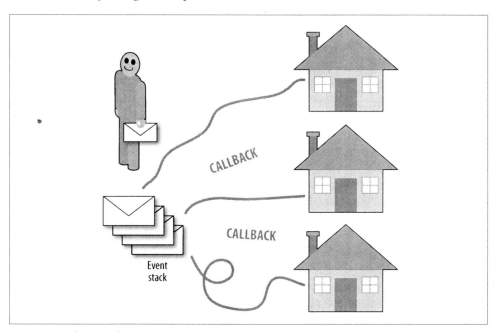

Figure 3-2. The event-loop postman

Sometimes, while the postman is walking a code route, someone will give him another letter. This is the callback function he is visiting at the moment. In this case, the postman delivers the new message immediately (after all, someone gave it to him directly instead of going via the post office, so it must be urgent). The postman will diverge from his current code path and walk the proper code path to deliver the new event. He then carries on walking the original code path emitted by the previous event.

Let's look at the behavior of our postman in a typical program by picking something simple. Suppose we have a web (HTTP) server that gets requests, retrieves some data from a database, and returns it to the user. In this scenario, we have a few events to deal with. First (as in most cases) comes the request event from the user asking the web server for a web page. The callback that deals with the initial request (let's call it callback A) looks at the request object and figures out what data it needs from the database. It then makes a request to the database for that data, passing another function, callback B, to be called on the response event. Having handled the request, callback A returns. When the database has found the data, it issues the response event. The event loop then calls callback B, which sends the data back to the user.

This seems fairly straightforward. The obvious thing to note here is the "break" in the code, which you wouldn't get in a procedural system. Because Node.js is a nonblocking system, when we get to the database call that would make us wait, we instead issue a callback. This means that different functions must start handling the request and finish handling it when the data is ready to return. So we need to make sure that we either pass any state we need to the callback or make it available in some other way. JavaScript programming typically does it through closures. We'll discuss that in more detail later.

Why does this make Node more efficient? Imagine ordering food at a fast food restaurant. When you get in line at the counter, the server taking your order can behave in two ways. One of them is event-driven, and one of them isn't. Let's start with the typical approach taken by PHP and many other web platforms. When you ask the server for your order, he takes it but won't serve any other customers until he has completed your order. There are a few things he can do after he's typed in your order: process your payment, pour your drink, and so on. However, the server is still going to have to wait an unknown amount of time for the kitchen to make your burger (one of us is vegetarian, and orders always seem to take ages). If, as in the traditional approach of web application frameworks, each server (thread) is allocated to just one request at a time, the only way to scale up is to add more threads. However, it's also very obvious that our server isn't being very efficient. He's spending a lot of time waiting for the kitchen to cook the food.

Obviously, real-life restaurants use a much more efficient model. When a server has finished taking your order, you receive a number that he can use to call you back. You could say this is a callback number. This is how Node works. When slow things such as I/O start, Node simply gives them a callback reference and then gets on with other work that is ready now, like the next customer (or event, in Node's case). It's important to note that as we saw in the example of the postman, at no time do restaurant servers ever deal with two customers at the same time. When they are calling someone back to collect an order, they are not taking a new one, and vice versa. By acting in an event-driven way, the servers are able to maximize their throughput.

This analogy also illustrates the cases where Node fits well and those where it doesn't. In a small restaurant where the kitchen staff and the wait staff are the same people, no improvement can be made by becoming event-driven. Because all the work is being done by the same people, event-driven architectures don't add anything. If all (or most) of the work your server does is computation, Node might not be the ideal model.

However, we can also see when the architecture fits. Imagine there are two servers and four customers in a restaurant (Figure 3-3). If the servers serve only one customer at a time, the first two customers will get the fastest possible order, but the third and fourth customers will get a terrible experience. The first two customers will get their food as soon as it is ready because the servers have dedicated their whole attention to fulfilling their orders. That comes at the cost of the other two customers. In an event-driven model, the first two customers might have to wait a short amount of time for the servers to finish taking the orders of the third and fourth customers before they get their food, but the average wait time (latency) of the system will be much, much lower.

Figure 3-3. Fast food, fast code

Let's look at another example. We've given the event-loop postman a letter to deliver that requires a gate to be opened. He gets there and the gate is closed, so he simply waits and tries again and again. He's trapped in an endless loop waiting for the gate to open (Figure 3-4). Perhaps there is a letter on the stack that will ask someone to open the gate so the postman can get through. Surely that will solve things, right? Unfortunately, this will only help if the postman gets to deliver the letter, and currently he's stuck waiting endlessly for the gate to open. This is because the event that opens the gate is external to the current event callback. If we emit the event from within a callback, we already know our postman will go and deliver that letter before carrying on, but when events are emitted outside the currently executing piece of code, they will not be called until that piece of code has been fully evaluated to its conclusion.

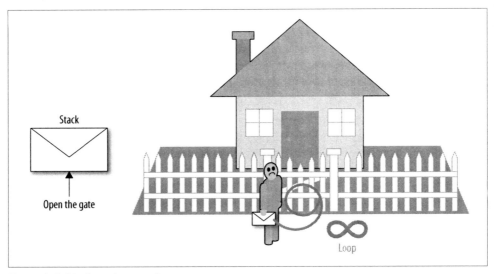

Figure 3-4. Blocking the event loop

As an illustration, the code in Example 3-1 creates a loop that Node.js (or a browser) will never break out of.

Example 3-1. Event-loop blocking code

```
EE = require('events').EventEmitter;
ee = new EE();

die = false;

ee.on('die', function() {
    die = true;
});

setTimeout(function() {
    ee.emit('die');
}, 100);

while(!die) {
}

console.log('done');
```

In this example, `console.log` will never be called, because the `while` loop stops Node from ever getting a chance to call back the timeout and emit the `die` event. Although it's unlikely we'd program a loop like this that relies on an external condition to exit, it illustrates how Node.js can do only one thing at once, and getting a fly in the ointment can really screw up the whole server. This is why nonblocking I/O is an essential part of event-driven programming.

Let's consider some numbers. When we run an operation in the CPU (not a line of JavaScript, but a single machine code operation), it takes about one-third of a nano-second (ns). A 3Ghz processor runs 3×10^9 instructions a second, so each instruction takes $10^{-9}/3$ seconds each. There are typically two types of memory in a CPU, L1 and L2 cache, each of which takes approximately 2–5ns to access. If we get data from memory (RAM), it takes about 80ns, which is about two orders of magnitude slower than running an instruction. However, all of these things are in the same ballpark. Getting things from slower forms of I/O is not quite so good. Imagine that getting data from RAM is equivalent to the weight of a cat. Retrieving data from the hard drive, then, could be considered to be the weight of a whale. Getting things from the network is like 100 whales. Think about how running `var foo = "bar"` versus a database query is a single cat versus 100 blue whales. Blocking I/O doesn't put an actual gate in front of the event-loop postman, but it does send him via Timbuktu when he is delivering his events.

Given a basic understanding of the event loop, let's look at the standard Node.js code for creating an HTTP server, shown in Example 3-2.

Example 3-2. A basic HTTP server

```
var http = require('http');
http.createServer(function (req, res) {
  res.writeHead(200, {'Content-Type': 'text/plain'});
  res.end('Hello World\n');
}).listen(8124, "127.0.0.1");
console.log('Server running at http://127.0.0.1:8124/');
```

This code is the most basic example from the Node.js website (but as we'll see soon, it's not the ideal way to code). The example creates an HTTP server using a factory method in the `http` library. The factory method creates a new HTTP server and attaches a callback to the `request` event. The callback is specified as the argument to the `crea teServer` method. What's interesting here is what happens when this code is run. The first thing Node.js does is run the code in the example from top to bottom. This can be considered the "setup" phase of Node programming. Because we attached some event listeners, Node.js doesn't exit, but instead waits for an event to be fired. If we didn't attach any events, Node.js would exit as soon as it had run the code.

So what happens when the server gets an HTTP request? Node.js emits the `request` event, which causes the callbacks attached to that event to be run in order. In this case, there is only one callback, the anonymous function we passed as an argument to `crea teServer`. Let's assume it's the first request the server has had since setup. Because there is no other code running, the `request` event is handled immediately and the callback is run. It's a very simple callback, and it runs pretty fast.

Let's assume that our site gets really popular and we get lots of requests. If, for the sake of argument, our callback takes 1 second and we get a second request shortly after the first one, the second request isn't going to be acted on for another second or so. Obviously, a second is a really long time, and as we look at the requirements of real-world applications, the problem of blocking the event loop becomes more damaging to the user experience. The operating system kernel actually handles the TCP connections to clients for the HTTP server, so there isn't a risk of rejecting new connections, but there is a real danger of not acting on them. The upshot of this is that we want to keep Node.js as event-driven and nonblocking as possible. In the same way that a slow I/O event should use callbacks to indicate the presence of data that Node.js can act on, the Node.js program itself should be written in such a way that no single callback ties up the event loop for extended periods of time.

This means that you should follow two strategies when writing a Node.js server:

- Once setup has been completed, make all actions event-driven.
- If Node.js is required to process something that will take a long time, consider delegating it to web workers.

Taking the event-driven approach works effectively with the event loop (the name is a hint that it would), but it's also important to write event-driven code in a way that is easy to read and understand. In the previous example, we used an anonymous function as the event callback, which makes things hard in a couple of ways. First, we have no control over where the code is used. An anonymous function's call stack starts from when it is used, rather than when the callback is attached to an event. This affects debugging. If everything is an anonymous event, it can be hard to distinguish similar callbacks when an exception occurs.

Patterns

Event-driven programming is different from procedural programming. The easiest way to learn it is to practice routine patterns that have been discovered by previous generations of programmers. That is the purpose of this section.

Before we launch into patterns, we'll take a look at what is really happening behind various programming styles to give the patterns some context. Most of this section will focus on I/O, because, as discussed in the previous section, event-driven programming is focused on solving problems with I/O. When it is working with data in memory that doesn't require I/O, Node can be completely procedural.

The I/O Problem Space

We'll start by looking at the types of I/O required in efficient systems. These will be the basis of our patterns.

The first obvious distinction to look at is serial versus parallel I/O. Serial is obvious: do *this* I/O, and after it is finished, do *that* I/O. Parallel is more complicated to implement but also easy to understand: do *this* I/O and *that* I/O at the same time. The important point here is that ordering is normally considered implicit in serial tasks, but parallel tasks could return in any order.

Groups of serial and parallel work can also be combined. For example, two groups of parallel requests could execute serially: do *this* and *that* together, then do *other* and *another* together.

In Node, we assume that all I/O has unbounded latency. This means that any I/O tasks could take from 0 to infinite time. We don't know, and can't assume, how long these tasks take. So instead of waiting for them, we use placeholders (events), which then fire callbacks when the I/O happens. Because we have assumed unbounded latency, it's easy to perform parallel tasks. You simply make a number of calls for various I/O tasks. They will return whenever they are ready, in whatever order that happens to be. Ordered serial requests are also easy to make by nesting or referencing callbacks together so that the first callback will initiate the second I/O request, the second callback will initiate the third, and so on. Even though each request is asynchronous and doesn't block the event loop, the requests are made in serial. This pattern of ordered requests is useful when the results of one I/O operation have to inform the details of the next I/O request.

So far, we have two ways to do I/O: ordered serial requests and unordered parallel requests. Ordered parallel requests are also a useful pattern; they happen when we allow the I/O to take place in parallel, but we deal with the results in a particular sequence. Unordered serial I/O offers no particular benefits, so we won't consider it as a pattern.

Unordered parallel I/O

Let's start with unordered parallel I/O (Example 3-3) because it's by far the easiest to do in Node. In fact, all I/O in Node is unordered parallel by default. This is because all I/O in Node is asynchronous and nonblocking. When we do any I/O, we simply throw the request out there and see what happens. It's possible that all the requests will happen in the order we made them, but maybe they won't. When we talk about unordered, we don't mean randomized, but simply that there is no guaranteed order.

Example 3-3. Unordered parallel I/O in Node

```
fs.readFile('foo.txt', 'utf8', function(err, data) {
  console.log(data);
};
fs.readFile('bar.txt', 'utf8', function(err, data) {
  console.log(data);
};
```

Simply making I/O requests with callbacks will create unordered parallel I/O. At some point in the future, both of these callbacks will fire. Which happens first is unknown, and either one could return an error rather than data without affecting the other request.

Ordered serial I/O

In this pattern, we want to do some I/O (unbounded latency) tasks in sequence. Each previous task must be completed before the next task is started. In Node, this means nesting callbacks so that the callback from each task starts the next task, as shown in Example 3-4.

Example 3-4. Nesting callbacks to produce serial requests

```
server.on('request', function(req, res) {
  //get session information from memcached
  memcached.getSession(req, function(session) {
    //get information from db
    db.get(session.user, function(userData) {
      //some other web service call
      ws.get(req, function(wsData) {
        //render page
        page = pageRender(req, session, userData, wsData);
        //output the response
        res.write(page);
      });
    });
  });
});
```

Although nesting callbacks allows easy creation of ordered serial I/O, it also creates so-called "pyramid" code.[1] This code can be hard to read and understand, and as a consequence, hard to maintain. For instance, a glance at Example 3-4 doesn't reveal that the completion of the `memcached.getSession` request launches the `db.get` request, that the completion of the `db.get` request launches the `ws.get` request, and so on. There are a few ways to make this code more readable without breaking the fundamental ordered serial pattern.

First, we can continue to use inline function declarations, but we can name them, as in Example 3-5. This makes debugging a lot easier as well as giving an indication of what the callback is going to do.

Example 3-5. Naming function calls in callbacks

```
server.on('request', getMemCached(req, res) {
  memcached.getSession(req, getDbInfo(session) {
    db.get(session.user, getWsInfo(userData) {
      ws.get(req, render(wsData) {
        //render page
        page = pageRender(req, session, userData, wsData);
        //output the response
        res.write(page);
      });
    });
```

---

1. This term was coined by Tim Caswell.

```
  });
});
```

Another approach that changes the style of code is to use declared functions instead of just anonymous or named ones. This removes the natural pyramid seen in the other approaches, which shows the order of execution, but it also breaks the code out into more manageable chunks (see Example 3-6).

Example 3-6. Using declared functions to separate out code

```
var render = function(wsData) {
  page = pageRender(req, session, userData, wsData);
};

var getWsInfo = function(userData) {
  ws.get(req, render);
};

var getDbInfo = function(session) {
  db.get(session.user, getWsInfo);
};

var getMemCached = function(req, res) {
  memcached.getSession(req, getDbInfo);
};
```

The code shown in this example won't actually work. The original nested code used closures to encapsulate some variables and make them available to subsequent functions. Hence, declared functions can be good when state doesn't need to be maintained across three or more callbacks. If you need only the information from the last callback in order to do the next one, it works well. It can be a lot more readable (especially with documentation) than a huge lump of nested functions.

There are, of course, ways of passing data around between functions. Mostly it comes down to using the features of the JavaScript language itself. JavaScript has functional scope, which means that when you declare var within a function, the variable becomes local to that function. However, simply having { and } does not limit the scope of a variable. This allows us to define variables in the outer callback that can be accessed by the inner callbacks even when the outer callbacks have "closed" by returning. When we nest callbacks, we are implicitly binding the variables from all the previous callbacks into the most recently defined callback. It just turns out that lots of nesting isn't very easy to work with.

We can still perform the flattening refactoring we did, but we should do it within the shared scope of the original request, to form a closure environment around all the callbacks we want to do. This way, all the callbacks relating to that initial request can be encapsulated and can share state via variables in the encapsulating callback (Example 3-7).

Example 3-7. Encapsulating within a callback

```
    server.on('request', function(req, res) {

  var render = function(wsData) {
    page = pageRender(req, session, userData, wsData);
  };

  var getWsInfo = function(userData) {
    ws.get(req, render);
  };

  var getDbInfo = function(session) {
    db.get(session.user, getWsInfo);
  };

  var getMemCached = function(req, res) {
    memcached.getSession(req, getDbInfo);
  };

}
```

Not only does this approach organize code in a logical way, but it also allows you to flatten a lot of the callback hell.

Other organizational innovations are also possible. Sometimes there is code you want to reuse across many functions. This is the province of *middleware*. There are many ways to do middleware. One of the most popular in Node is the model used by the Connect framework, which could be said to be based on Rack from the Ruby world. The general idea behind its implementation is that we pass around some variables that represent not only the state but also the methods of interacting with that state.

In JavaScript, objects are passed by reference. That means when you call `my Function(someObject)`, any changes you make to `someObject` will affect all copies of `someObject` in your current functional scope. This is potentially tricky, but gives you some great powers if you are careful about any side effects created. Side effects are largely dangerous in asynchronous code. When something modifies an object used by a callback, it can often be very difficult to figure out when that change happened because it happens in a nonlinear order. If you use the ability to change objects passed by arguments, be considerate of where those objects are going to be used.

The basic idea is to take something that represents the state and pass it between all functions that need to act on that state. This means that all the things acting on the state need to have the same interface so they can pass between themselves. This is why Connect (and therefore Express) middleware all takes the form `function(req, res, next)`. We discuss Connect/Express middleware in more detail in Chapter 7.

In the meantime, let's look at the basic approach, shown in Example 3-8. When we share objects between functions, earlier functions in the call stack can affect the state of those objects such that the later objects utilize the changes.

Example 3-8. Passing changes between functions

```
      var AwesomeClass = function() {
  this.awesomeProp = 'awesome!'
  this.awesomeFunc = function(text) {
    console.log(text + ' is awesome!')
  }
}

var awesomeObject = new AwesomeClass()

function middleware(func) {
  oldFunc = func.awesomeFunc
  func.awesomeFunc = function(text) {
    text = text + ' really'
    oldFunc(text)
  }
}

function anotherMiddleware(func) {
  func.anotherProp = 'super duper'
}

function caller(input) {
  input.awesomeFunc(input.anotherProp)
}

middleware(awesomeObject)
anotherMiddleware(awesomeObject)
caller(awesomeObject)
```

Writing Code for Production

One of the challenges of writing a book is trying to explain things in the simplest way possible. That runs counter to showing techniques and functional code that you'd want to deploy. Although we should always strive to have the simplest, most understandable code possible, sometimes you need to do things that make code more robust or faster at the cost of making it less simple. This section provides guidance about how to harden the applications you deploy, which you can take with you as you explore upcoming chapters. This section is about writing code with maturity that will keep your application running long into the future. It's not exhaustive, but if you write robust code, you won't have to deal with so many maintenance issues. One of the trade-offs of Node's single-threaded approach is a tendency to be brittle. These techniques help mitigate this risk.

Deploying a production application is not the same as running test programs on your laptop. Servers can have a wide variety of resource constraints, but they tend to have a lot more resources than the typical machine you would develop on. Typically, frontend servers have many more cores (CPUs) than laptop or desktop machines, but less hard drive space. They also have a lot of RAM. Node currently has some constraints, such as a maximum JavaScript heap size. This affects the way you deploy because you want to maximize the use of the CPUs and memory on the machine while using Node's easy-to-program single-threaded approach.

Error Handling

As we saw earlier in this chapter, you can split I/O activities from other things in Node, and error handling is one of those things. JavaScript includes try/catch functionality, but it's appropriate only for errors that happen inline. When you do nonblocking I/O in Node, you pass a callback to the function. This means the callback is going to run when the event happens outside of the try/catch block. We need to be able to provide error handling that works in asynchronous situations. Consider the code in Example 3-9.

Example 3-9. Trying to catch an error in a callback and failing

```
var http = require('http')

var opts = {
  host: 'sfnsdkfjdsnk.com',
  port: 80,
  path: '/'
}

try {
  http.get(opts, function(res) {
    console.log('Will this get called?')
  })
}
catch (e) {
  console.log('Will we catch an error?')
}
```

When you call `http.get()`, what is actually happening? We pass some parameters specifying the I/O we want to happen and a callback function. When the I/O completes, the callback function will be fired. However, the `http.get()` call will succeed simply by issuing the callback. An error during the GET cannot be caught by a try/catch block.

The disconnect from I/O errors is even more obvious in Node REPL. Because the REPL shell prints out any return values that are not assigned, we can see that the return value of calling `http.get()` is the `http.ClientRequest` object that is created. This means that the try/catch did its job by making sure the specified code returned without errors. However, because the hostname is nonsense, a problem will occur within this I/O request. This means the callback can't be completed successfully. A try/catch can't help with this, because the error has happened outside the JavaScript, and when Node is ready to report it, we are not in that call stack any more. We've moved on to dealing with another event.

We deal with this in Node by using the error event. This is a special event that is fired when an error occurs. It allows a module engaging in I/O to fire an alternative event to the one the callback was listening for to deal with the error. The error event allows us to deal with any errors that might occur in any of the callbacks that happen in any modules we use. Let's write the previous example correctly, as shown in Example 3-10.

Example 3-10. Catching an I/O error with the error event

```
var http = require('http')

var opts = {
  host: 'dskjvnfskcsjsdkcds.net',
  port: 80,
  path: '/'
}

var req = http.get(opts, function(res) {
  console.log('This will never get called')
})

req.on('error', function(e) {
  console.log('Got that pesky error trapped')
})
```

By using the error event, we got to deal with the error (in this case by ignoring it). However, our program survived, which is the main thing. Like try/catch in JavaScript, the error event catches all kinds of exceptions. A good general approach to exception handling is to set up conditionals to check for known error conditions and deal with them if possible. Otherwise, catching any remaining errors, logging them, and keeping your server running is probably the best approach.

Using Multiple Processors

As we've mentioned, Node is single-threaded. This means Node is using only one processor to do its work. However, most servers have several "multicore" processors, and a single multicore processor has many processors. A server with two physical CPU sockets might have "24 logical cores"—that is, 24 processors exposed to the operating system. To make the best use of Node, we should use those too. So if we don't have threads, how do we do that?

Node provides a module called cluster that allows you to delegate work to child processes. This means that Node creates a copy of its current program in another process (on Windows, it is actually another thread). Each child process has some special abilities, such as the ability to share a socket with other children. This allows us to write Node programs that start many other Node programs and then delegate work to them.

It is important to understand that when you use cluster to share work between a number of copies of a Node program, the master process isn't involved in every transaction. The master process manages the child processes, but when the children interact with I/O they do it directly, not through the master. This means that if you set up a web server using cluster, requests don't go through your master process, but directly to the children. Hence, dispatching requests does not create a bottleneck in the system.

By using the cluster API, you can distribute work to a Node process on every available core of your server. This makes the best use of the resource. Let's look at a simple cluster script in Example 3-11.

Example 3-11. Using cluster to distribute work

```
var cluster = require('cluster');
var http = require('http');
var numCPUs = require('os').cpus().length;

if (cluster.isMaster) {
  // Fork workers.
  for (var i = 0; i < numCPUs; i++) {
    cluster.fork();
  }

  cluster.on('death', function(worker) {
    console.log('worker ' + worker.pid + ' died');
  });
} else {
  // Worker processes have a http server.
  http.Server(function(req, res) {
    res.writeHead(200);
    res.end("hello world\n");
  }).listen(8000);
}
```

In this example, we use a few parts of Node core to evenly distribute the work across all of the CPUs available: the cluster module, the http module, and the os module. From the latter, we simply get the number of CPUs on the system.

The way cluster works is that each Node process becomes either a "master" or a "worker" process. When a master process calls the cluster.fork() method, it creates a child process that is identical to the master, except for two attributes that each process can check to see whether it is a master or child. In the master process—the one in which the script has been directly invoked by calling it with Node—cluster.isMaster returns true, whereas cluster.isWorker returns false. cluster.isMaster returns false on the child, whereas cluster.isWorker returns true.

The example shows a master script that invokes a worker for each CPU. Each child starts an HTTP server, which is another unique aspect of cluster. When you lis ten() to a socket where cluster is in use, many processes can listen to the same socket. If you simply started serveral Node processes with node myscript.js, this wouldn't be possible, because the second process to start would throw the EADDRINUSE exception. cluster provides a cross-platform way to invoke several processes that share a socket. And even when the children all share a connection to a port, if one of them is jammed, it doesn't stop the other workers from getting connections.

We can do more with `cluster` than simply share sockets, because it is based on the `child_process` module. This gives us a number of attributes, and some of the most useful ones relate to the health of the child processes. In the previous example, when a child dies, the master process uses `console.log()` to print out a death notification. However, a more useful script would `cluster.fork()` a new child, as shown in Example 3-12.

Example 3-12. Forking a new worker when a death occurs

```
    if (cluster.isMaster) {
  //Fork workers.
  for (var i=0; i<numCPUs; i++) {
    cluster.fork();
  }

  cluster.on('death', function(worker) {
    console.log('worker ' + worker.pid + ' died');
    cluster.fork();
  });
}
```

This simple change means that our master process can keep restarting dying processes to keep our server firing on all CPUs. However, this is just a basic check for running processes. We can also do some more fancy tricks. Because workers can pass messages to the master, we can have each worker report some stats, such as memory usage, to the master. This will allow the master to determine when workers are becoming unruly or to confirm that workers are not freezing or getting stuck in long-running events (see Example 3-13).

Example 3-13. Monitoring worker health using message passing

```
var cluster = require('cluster');
var http = require('http');
var numCPUs = require('os').cpus().length;

var rssWarn = (12 * 1024 * 1024)
  , heapWarn = (10 * 1024 * 1024)

if(cluster.isMaster) {
  for(var i=0; i<numCPUs; i++) {
    var worker = cluster.fork();
    worker.on('message', function(m) {
      if (m.memory) {
        if(m.memory.rss > rssWarn) {
          console.log('Worker ' + m.process + ' using too much memory.')
        }
      }
    })
  }
} else {
  //Server
  http.Server(function(req,res) {
```

```
    res.writeHead(200);
    res.end('hello world\n')
  }).listen(8000)
  //Report stats once a second
  setInterval(function report(){
    process.send({memory: process.memoryUsage(), process: process.pid});
  }, 1000)
}
```

In this example, workers report on their memory usage, and the master sends an alert to the log when a process uses too much memory. This replicates the functionality of many health reporting systems that operations teams already use. It gives control to the master Node process, however, which has some benefits. This message-passing interface allows the master process to send messages back to the workers too. This means you can treat a master process as a lightly loaded admin interface to your workers.

There are other things we can do with message passing that we can't do from the outside of Node. Because Node relies on an event loop to do its work, there is the danger that the callback of an event in the loop could run for a long time. This means that other users of the process are not going to get their requests met until that long-running event's callback has concluded. The master process has a connection to each worker, so we can tell it to expect an "all OK" notification periodically. This means we can validate that the event loop has the appropriate amount of turnover and that it hasn't become stuck on one callback. Sadly, identifying a long-running callback doesn't allow us to make a callback for termination. Because any notification we could send to the process will get added to the event queue, it would have to wait for the long-running callback to finish. Consequently, although using the master process allows us to identify zombie workers, our only remedy is to kill the worker and lose all the tasks it was doing.

Some preparation can give you the capability to kill an individual worker that threatens to take over its processor; see Example 3-14.

Example 3-14. Killing zombie workers

```
var cluster = require('cluster');
var http = require('http');
var numCPUs = require('os').cpus().length;

var rssWarn = (50 * 1024 * 1024)
  , heapWarn = (50 * 1024 * 1024)

var workers = {}

if(cluster.isMaster) {
  for(var i=0; i<numCPUs; i++) {
    createWorker()
  }
```

```
    setInterval(function() {
      var time = new Date().getTime()
      for(pid in workers) {
        if(workers.hasOwnProperty(pid) &&
           workers[pid].lastCb + 5000 < time) {

          console.log('Long running worker ' + pid + ' killed')
          workers[pid].worker.kill()
          delete workers[pid]
          createWorker()
        }
      }
    }, 1000)
} else {
  //Server
  http.Server(function(req,res) {
    //mess up 1 in 200 reqs
    if (Math.floor(Math.random() * 200) === 4) {
      console.log('Stopped ' + process.pid + ' from ever finishing')
      while(true) { continue }
    }
    res.writeHead(200);
    res.end('hello world from ' + process.pid + '\n')
  }).listen(8000)
  //Report stats once a second
  setInterval(function report(){
    process.send({cmd: "reportMem", memory: process.memoryUsage(), process: process.pid})
  }, 1000)
}

function createWorker() {
  var worker = cluster.fork()
  console.log('Created worker: ' + worker.pid)
  //allow boot time
  workers[worker.pid] = {worker:worker, lastCb: new Date().getTime()-1000}
  worker.on('message', function(m) {
    if(m.cmd === "reportMem") {
      workers[m.process].lastCb = new Date().getTime()
      if(m.memory.rss > rssWarn) {
        console.log('Worker ' + m.process + ' using too much memory.')
      }
    }
  })
}
```

In this script, we've added an interval to the master as well as the workers. Now whenever a worker sends a report to the master process, the master stores the time of the report. Every second or so, the master process looks at all its workers to check whether any of them haven't responded in longer than 5 seconds (using > 5000 because timeouts are in milliseconds). If that is the case, it kills the stuck worker and restarts it. To make this process effective, we moved the creation of workers into a small function. This allows us to do the various pieces of setup in a single place, regardless of whether we are creating a new worker or restarting a dead one.

We also made a small change to the HTTP server in order to give each request a 1 in 200 chance of failing, so you can run the script and see what it's like to get failures. If you do a bunch of parallel requests from several sources, you'll see the way this works. These are all entirely separate Node programs that interact via message passing, which means that no matter what happens, the master process can check on the other processes because the master is a small program that won't get jammed.

## PART II

Deep Dive and API Reference

## CHAPTER 4

Core APIs

There are a lot of APIs in Node, but some of them are more important than others. These core APIs will form the backbone of any Node app, and you'll find yourself using them again and again.

Events

The first API we are going to look at is the Events API. This is because, while abstract, it is a fundamental piece of making every other API work. By having a good grip on this API, you'll be able to use all the other APIs effectively.

If you've ever programmed JavaScript in the browser, you'll have used events before. However, the event model used in the browser comes from the DOM rather than Java-Script itself, and a lot of the concepts in the DOM don't necessarily make sense out of that context. Let's look at the DOM model of events and compare it to the implementation in Node.

The DOM has a user-driven event model based on user interaction, with a set of interface elements arranged in a tree structure (HTML, XML, etc.). This means that when a user interacts with a particular part of the interface, there is an event and a context, which is the HTML/XML element on which the click or other activity took place. That context has a parent and potentially children. Because the context is within a tree, the model includes the concepts of bubbling and capturing, which allow elements either up or down the tree to receive the event that was called.

For example, in an HTML list, a click event on an <li> can be captured by a listener on the <ul> that is its parent. Conversely, a click on the <ul> can be bubbled down to a listener on the <li>. Because JavaScript objects don't have this kind of tree structure, the model in Node is much simpler.

EventEmitter

Because the event model is tied to the DOM in browsers, Node created the Event Emitter class to provide some basic event functionality. All event functionality in Node revolves around EventEmitter because it is also designed to be an interface class for other classes to extend. It would be unusual to call an EventEmitter instance directly.

EventEmitter has a handful of methods, the main two being on and emit. The class provides these methods for use by other classes. The on method creates an event listener for an event, as shown in Example 4-1.

Example 4-1. Listening for an event with the on method

```
server.on('event', function(a, b, c) {
  //do things
});
```

The on method takes two parameters: the name of the event to listen for and the function to call when that event is emitted. Because EventEmitter is an interface pseudoclass, the class that inherits from EventEmitter is expected to be invoked with the new keyword. Let's look at Example 4-2 to see how we create a new class as a listener.

Example 4-2. Creating a new class that supports events with EventEmitter

```
var utils = require('utils'),
    EventEmitter = require('events').EventEmitter;

var Server = function() {
  console.log('init');
};

utils.inherits(Server, EventEmitter);

var s = new Server();

s.on('abc', function() {
  console.log('abc');
});
```

We begin this example by including the utils module so we can use the inherits method. inherits provides a way for the EventEmitter class to add its methods to the Server class we created. This means all new instances of Server can be used as Event Emitters.

We then include the events module. However, we want to access just the specific EventEmitter class inside that module. Note how EventEmitter is capitalized to show it is a class. We didn't use a createEventEmitter method, because we aren't planning to use an EventEmitter directly. We simply want to attach its methods to the Server class we are going to make.

Once we have included the modules we need, the next step is to create our basic Server class. This offers just one simple function, which logs a message when it is initialized. In a real implementation, we would decorate the Server class prototype with the functions that the class would use. For the sake of simplicity, we've skipped that. The important step is to use sys.inherits to add EventEmitter as a superclass of our Server class.

When we want to use the Server class, we instantiate it with new Server(). This instance of Server will have access to the methods in the superclass (EventEmitter), which means we can add a listener to our instance using the on method.

Right now, however, the event listener we added will never be called, because the abc event isn't fired. We can fix this by adding the code in Example 4-3 to emit the event.

Example 4-3. Emitting an event

```
s.emit('abc');
```

Firing the event listener is as simple as calling the emit method that the Server instance inherited from EventEmitter. It's important to note that these events are instance-based. There are no *global* events. When you call the on method, you attach to a specific EventEmitter-based object. Even the various instances of the Server class don't share events. s from the code in Example 4-3 will not share the same events as another Server instance, such as one created by var z = new Server();.

Callback Syntax

An important part of using events is dealing with callbacks. Chapter 3 looks at best practices in much more depth, but we'll look here at the mechanics of callbacks in Node. They use a few standard patterns, but first let's discuss what is possible.

When calling emit, in addition to the event name, you can also pass an arbitrary list of parameters. Example 4-4 includes three such parameters. These will be passed to the function listening to the event. When you receive a request event from the http server, for example, you receive two parameters: req and res. When the request event was emitted, those parameters were passed as the second and third arguments to the emit.

Example 4-4. Passing parameters when emitting an event

```
s.emit('abc', a, b, c);
```

It is important to understand how Node calls the event listeners because it will affect your programming style. When emit() is called with arguments, the code in Example 4-5 is used to call each event listener.

Example 4-5. Calling event listeners from emit

```
if (arguments.length <= 3) {
  // fast case
```

```
  handler.call(this, arguments[1], arguments[2]);
} else {
  // slower
  var args = Array.prototype.slice.call(arguments, 1);
  handler.apply(this, args);
}
```

This code uses both of the JavaScript methods for calling a function from code. If
emit() is passed with three or fewer arguments, the method takes a shortcut and uses
call. Otherwise, it uses the slower apply to pass all the arguments as an array. The
important thing to recognize here, though, is that Node makes both of these calls using
the this argument directly. This means that the context in which the event listeners are
called is the context of EventEmitter—*not* their original context. Using Node REPL,
you can see what is happening when things get called by EventEmitter (Example 4-6).

Example 4-6. The changes in context caused by EventEmitter

```
> var EventEmitter = require('events').EventEmitter,
...      util = require('util');
>
> var Server = function() {};
> util.inherits(Server, EventEmitter);
> Server.prototype.outputThis= function(output) {
...    console.log(this);
...    console.log(output);
... };
[Function]
>
> Server.prototype.emitOutput = function(input) {
...    this.emit('output', input);
... };
[Function]
>
> Server.prototype.callEmitOutput = function() {
...    this.emitOutput('innerEmitOutput');
... };
[Function]
>
> var s = new Server();
> s.on('output', s.outputThis);
{ _events: { output: [Function] } }
> s.emitOutput('outerEmitOutput');
{ _events: { output: [Function] } }
outerEmitOutput
> s.callEmitOutput();
{ _events: { output: [Function] } }
innerEmitOutput
> s.emit('output', 'Direct');
{ _events: { output: [Function] } }
Direct
true
>
```

The sample output first sets up a Server class. It includes functions to emit the output event. The outputThis method is attached to the output event as an event listener. When we emit the output event from various contexts, we stay within the scope of the EventEmitter object, so the value of this that s.outputThis has access to is the one belonging to the EventEmitter. Consequently, the this variable must be passed in as a parameter and assigned to a variable if we wish to make use of it in event callback functions.

HTTP

One of the core tasks of Node.js is to act as a web server. This is such a key part of the system that when Ryan Dahl started the project, he rewrote the HTTP stack for V8 to make it nonblocking. Although both the API and the internals for the original HTTP implementation have morphed a lot since it was created, the core activities are still the same. The Node implementation of HTTP is nonblocking and fast. Much of the code has moved from C into JavaScript.

HTTP uses a pattern that is common in Node. Pseudoclass factories provide an easy way to create a new server.[1] The http.createServer() method provides us with a new instance of the HTTP Server class, which is the class we use to define the actions taken when Node receives incoming HTTP requests. There are a few other main pieces of the HTTP module and other Node modules in general. These are the events the Server class fires and the data structures that are passed to the callbacks. Knowing about these three types of class allows you to use the HTTP module well.

HTTP Servers

Acting as an HTTP server is probably the most common current use case for Node. In Chapter 1, we set up an HTTP server and used it to serve a very simple request. However, HTTP is a lot more multifaceted than that. The server component of the HTTP module provides the raw tools to build complex and comprehensive web servers. In this chapter, we are going to explore the mechanics of dealing with requests and issuing responses. Even if you end up using a higher-level server such as Express, many of the concepts it uses are extensions of those defined here.

As we've already seen, the first step in using HTTP servers is to create a new server using the http.createServer() method. This returns a new instance of the Server class, which has only a few methods because most of the functionality is going to be provided through using events. The http server class has six events and three methods. The other thing to notice is how most of the methods are used to initialize the server, whereas events are used during its operation.

---

1. When we talk about a *pseudoclass,* we are referring to the definition found in Douglas Crockford's *JavaScript: The Good Parts* (O'Reilly). From now on, we will use "class" to refer to a "pseudoclass."

Let's start by creating the smallest basic HTTP server code we can in Example 4-7.

Example 4-7. A simple, and very short, HTTP server

```
require('http').createServer(function(req,res){res.writeHead(200, {});
res.end('hello world');}).listen(8125);
```

This example is *not* good code. However, it illustrates some important points. We'll fix the style shortly. The first thing we do is `require` the `http` module. Notice how we can chain methods to access the module without first assigning it to a variable. Many things in Node return a function,[2] which allows us to invoke those functions immediately. From the included `http` module, we call `createServer`. This doesn't have to take any arguments, but we pass it a function to attach to the `request` event. Finally, we tell the server created with `createServer` to `listen` on port 8125.

We hope you never write code like this in real situations, but it does show the flexibility of the syntax and the potential brevity of the language. Let's be a lot more explicit about our code. The rewrite in Example 4-8 should make it a lot easier to understand and maintain.

Example 4-8. A simple, but more descriptive, HTTP server

```
var http = require('http');
var server = http.createServer();
var handleReq = function(req,res){
  res.writeHead(200, {});
  res.end('hello world');
};
server.on('request', handleReq);
server.listen(8125);
```

This example implements the minimal web server again. However, we've started assigning things to named variables. This not only makes the code easier to read than when it's chained, but also means you can reuse it. For example, it's not uncommon to use `http` more than once in a file. You want to have both an HTTP server and an HTTP client, so reusing the module object is really helpful. Even though JavaScript doesn't force you to think about memory, that doesn't mean you should thoughtlessly litter unnecessary objects everywhere. So rather than use an anonymous callback, we've named the function that handles the `request` event. This is less about memory usage and more about readability. We're not saying you shouldn't use anonymous functions, but if you can lay out your code so it's easy to find, that helps a lot when maintaining it.

 Remember to look at Part I of the book for more help with programming style. Chapters 1 and 2 deal with programming style in particular.

---

2. This works in JavaScript because it supports first-class functions.

Because we didn't pass the request event listener as part of the factory method for the http Server object, we need to add an event listener explicitly. Calling the on method from EventEmitter does this. Finally, as with the previous example, we call the listen method with the port we want to listen on. The http class provides other functions, but this example illustrates the most important ones.

The http server supports a number of events, which are associated with either the TCP or HTTP connection to the client. The connection and close events indicate the buildup or teardown of a TCP connection to a client. It's important to remember that some clients will be using HTTP 1.1, which supports keepalive. This means that their TCP connections may remain open across multiple HTTP requests.

The request, checkContinue, upgrade, and clientError events are associated with HTTP requests. We've already used the request event, which signals a new HTTP request.

The checkContinue event indicates a special event. It allows you to take more direct control of an HTTP request in which the client streams chunks of data to the server. As the client sends data to the server, it will check whether it can continue, at which point this event will fire. If an event handler is created for this event, the request event will *not* be emitted.

The upgrade event is emitted when a client asks for a protocol upgrade. The http server will deny HTTP upgrade requests unless there is an event handler for this event.

Finally, the clientError event passes on any error events sent by the client.

The HTTP server can throw a few events. The most common one is request, but you can also get events associated with the TCP connection for the request as well as other parts of the request life cycle.

When a new TCP stream is created for a request, a connection event is emitted. This event passes the TCP stream for the request as a parameter. The stream is also available as a request.connection variable for each request that happens through it. However, only one connection event will be emitted for each stream. This means that many requests can happen from a client with only one connection event.

HTTP Clients

Node is also great when you want to make outgoing HTTP connections. This is useful in many contexts, such as using web services, connecting to document store databases, or just scraping websites. You can use the same http module when doing HTTP requests, but should use the http.ClientRequest class. There are two factory methods for this class: a general-purpose one and a convenience method. Let's take a look at the general-purpose case in Example 4-9.

Example 4-9. Creating an HTTP request

```
var http = require('http');

var opts = {
  host: 'www.google.com'
  port: 80,
  path: '/',
  method: 'GET'
};

var req = http.request(opts, function(res) {
  console.log(res);
  res.on('data', function(data) {
    console.log(data);
  });
});

req.end();
```

The first thing you can see is that an `options` object defines a lot of the functionality of the request. We must provide the `host` name (although an IP address is also acceptable), the `port`, and the `path`. The `method` is optional and defaults to a value of GET if none is specified. In essence, the example is specifying that the request should be an HTTP GET request to http://www.google.com/ on port 80.

The next thing we do is use the `options` object to construct an instance of `http.ClientRequest` using the factory method `http.request()`. This method takes an `options` object and an optional callback argument. The passed callback listens to the `response` event, and when a `response` event is received, we can process the results of the request. In the previous example, we simply output the response object to the console. However, it's important to notice that the body of the HTTP request is actually received via a stream in the `response` object. Thus, you can subscribe to the `data` event of the `response` object to get the data as it becomes available (see the section "Readable streams" on page 68 for more information).

The final important point to notice is that we had to `end()` the `request`. Because this was a GET request, we didn't write any data to the server, but for other HTTP methods, such as PUT or POST, you may need to. Until we call the `end()` method, `request` won't initiate the HTTP request, because it doesn't know whether it should still be waiting for us to send data.

Making HTTP GET requests

Since GET is such a common HTTP use case, there is a special factory method to support it in a more convenient way, as shown in Example 4-10.

Example 4-10. Simple HTTP GET requests

```
var http = require('http');

var opts = {
  host: 'www.google.com'
  port: 80,
  path: '/',
};

var req = http.get(opts, function(res) {
  console.log(res);
  res.on('data', function(data) {
    console.log(data);
  });
});
```

This example of `http.get()` does exactly the same thing as the previous example, but it's slightly more concise. We've lost the `method` attribute of the config object, and left out the call `request.end()` because it's implied.

If you run the previous two examples, you are going to get back raw `Buffer` objects. As described later in this chapter, a `Buffer` is a special class defined in Node to support the storage of arbitrary, binary data. Although it's certainly possible to work with these, you often want a specific encoding, such as UTF-8 (an encoding for Unicode characters). You can specify this with the `response.setEncoding()` method (see Example 4-11).

Example 4-11. Comparing raw Buffer output to output with a specified encoding

```
> var http = require('http');
> var req = http.get({host:'www.google.com', port:80, path:'/'}, function(res) {
... console.log(res);
... res.on('data', function(c) { console.log(c); });
... });
> <Buffer 3c 21 64 6f 63 74 79 70

...

65 2e 73 74>
<Buffer 61 72 74 54 69

...

69 70 74 3e>

>
> var req = http.get({host:'www.google.com', port:80, path:'/'}, function(res) {
... res.setEncoding('utf8');
... res.on('data', function(c) { console.log(c); });
... });
> <!doctype html><html><head><meta http-equiv="content-type

...
```

```
load.t.prt=(f=(new Date).getTime());
})();
</script>


>
```

In the first case, we do not pass ClientResponse.setEncoding(), and we get chunks of data in Buffers. Although the output is abridged in the printout, you can see that it isn't just a single Buffer, but that several Buffers have been returned with data. In the second example, the data is returned as UTF-8 because we specified res.setEncod ing('utf8'). The chunks of data returned from the server are still the same, but are given to the program as strings in the correct encoding rather than as raw Buffers. Although the printout may not make this clear, there is one string for each of the original Buffers.

Uploading data for HTTP POST and PUT

Not all HTTP is GET. You might also need to call POST, PUT, and other HTTP methods that alter data on the other end. This is functionally the same as making a GET request, except you are going to write some data *upstream*, as shown in Example 4-12.

Example 4-12. Writing data to an upstream service

```
var options = {
  host: 'www.example.com',
  port: 80,
  path: '/submit',
  method: 'POST'
};

var req = http.request(options, function(res) {
  res.setEncoding('utf8');
  res.on('data', function (chunk) {
    console.log('BODY: ' + chunk);
  });
});

req.write("my data");
req.write("more of my data");

req.end();
```

This example is very similar to Example 4-10, but uses the http.ClientRequest .write() method. This method allows you to send data upstream, and as explained earlier, it requires you to explicitly call http.ClientRequest.end() to indicate you're finished sending data. Whenever ClientRequest.write() is called, the data is sent upstream (it isn't buffered), but the server will not respond until ClientRequest.end() is called.

You can stream data to a server using `ClientRequest.write()` by coupling the writes to the `data` event of a `Stream`. This is ideal if you need to, for example, send a file from disk to a remote server over HTTP.

The ClientResponse object

The `ClientResponse` object stores a variety of information about the request. In general, it is pretty intuitive. Some of its obvious properties that are often useful include `statusCode` (which contains the HTTP status) and `header` (which is the response header object). Also hung off of `ClientResponse` are various streams and properties that you may or may not want to interact with directly.

URL

The `URL` module provides tools for easily parsing and dealing with URL strings. It's extremely useful when you have to deal with URLs. The module offers three methods: `parse`, `format`, and `resolve`. Let's start by looking at Example 4-13, which demonstrates `parse` using Node REPL.

Example 4-13. Parsing a URL using the URL module

```
> var URL = require('url');
> var myUrl = "http://www.nodejs.org/some/url/?with=query&param=that&are=awesome
#alsoahash";
> myUrl
'http://www.nodejs.org/some/url/?with=query&param=that&are=awesome#alsoahash'
> parsedUrl = URL.parse(myUrl);
{ href: 'http://www.nodejs.org/some/url/?with=query&param=that&are=awesome#alsoahash'
, protocol: 'http:'
, slashes: true
, host: 'www.nodejs.org'
, hostname: 'www.nodejs.org'
, hash: '#alsoahash'
, search: '?with=query&param=that&are=awesome'
, query: 'with=query&param=that&are=awesome'
, pathname: '/some/url/'
}
> parsedUrl = URL.parse(myUrl, true);
{ href: 'http://www.nodejs.org/some/url/?with=query&param=that&are=awesome#alsoahash'
, protocol: 'http:'
, slashes: true
, host: 'www.nodejs.org'
, hostname: 'www.nodejs.org'
, hash: '#alsoahash'
, search: '?with=query&param=that&are=awesome'
, query:
  { with: 'query'
  , param: 'that'
  , are: 'awesome'
  }
```

```
, pathname: '/some/url/'
}
>
```

The first thing we do, of course, is require the URL module. Note that the names of modules are always lowercase. We've created a url as a string containing all the parts that will be parsed out. Parsing is really easy: we just call the parse method from the URL module on the string. It returns a data structure representing the parts of the parsed URL. The components it produces are:

- href
- protocol
- host
- auth
- hostname
- port
- pathname
- search
- query
- hash

The href is the full URL that was originally passed to parse. The protocol is the protocol used in the URL (e.g., http://, https://, ftp://, etc.). host is the fully qualified hostname of the URL. This could be as simple as the hostname for a local server, such as print server, or a fully qualified domain name such as www.google.com. It might also include a port number, such as 8080, or username and password credentials like un:pw@ftpserver.com. The various parts of the hostname are broken down further into auth, containing just the user credentials; port, containing just the port; and host name, containing the hostname portion of the URL. An important thing to know about hostname is that it is still the full hostname, including the top-level domain (TLD; e.g., .com, .net, etc.) and the specific server. If the URL were http://sport.yahoo.com/nhl, hostname would not give you just the TLD (yahoo.com) or just the host (sport), but the entire hostname (sport.yahoo.com). The URL module doesn't have the capability to split the hostname down into its components, such as domain or TLD.

The next set of components of the URL relates to everything after the host. The path name is the entire filepath after the host. In http://sports.yahoo.com/nhl, it is /nhl. The next component is the search component, which stores the HTTP GET parameters in the URL. For example, if the URL were http://mydomain.com/?foo=bar&baz=qux, the search component would be ?foo=bar&baz=qux. Note the inclusion of the ?. The query parameter is similar to the search component. It contains one of two things, depending on how parse was called.

parse takes two arguments: the `url` string and an optional Boolean that determines whether the `queryString` should be parsed using the `querystring` module, discussed in the next section. If the second argument is false, `query` will just contain a string similar to that of `search` but without the leading ?. If you don't pass anything for the second argument, it defaults to `false`.

The final component is the `fragment` portion of the URL. This is the part of the URL after the #. Commonly, this is used to refer to named anchors in `HTML` pages. For instance, `http://abook.com/#chapter2` might refer to the second chapter on a web page hosting a whole book. The `hash` component in this case would contain `#chapter2`. Again, note the included # in the string. Some sites, such as `http://twitter.com`, use more complex fragments for AJAX applications, but the same rules apply. So the URL for the Twitter *mentions* account, `http://twitter.com/#!/mentions`, would have a `path name` of / but a `hash` of `#!/mentions`.

querystring

The `querystring` module is a very simple helper module to deal with query strings. As discussed in the previous section, query strings are the parameters encoded at the end of a URL. However, when reported back as just a JavaScript string, the parameters are fiddly to deal with. The `querystring` module provides an easy way to create objects from the query strings. The main methods it offers are `parse` and `decode`, but some internal helper functions, —such as `escape`, `unescape`, `unescapeBuffer`, `encode`, and `stringify`, are also exposed. If you have a query string, you can use `parse` to turn it into an object, as shown in Example 4-14.

Example 4-14. Parsing a query string with the querystring module in Node REPL

```
> var qs = require('querystring');
> qs.parse('a=1&b=2&c=d');
{ a: '1', b: '2', c: 'd' }
>
```

Here, the class's `parse` function turns the query string into an object in which the properties are the keys and the values correspond to the ones in the query string. You should notice a few things, though. First, the numbers are returned as strings, not numbers. Because JavaScript is loosely typed and will coerce a string into a number in a numerical operation, this works pretty well. However, it's worth bearing in mind for those times when that coercion doesn't work.

Additionally, it's important to note that you must pass the query string without the leading ? that demarks it in the URL. A typical URL might look like `http://www.bobs discount.com/?item=304&location=san+francisco`. The query string starts with a ? to indicate where the filepath ends, but if you include the ? in the string you pass to `parse`, the first key will start with a ?, which is almost certainly not what you want.

This library is really useful in a bunch of contexts because query strings are used in situations other than URLs. When you get content from an HTTP POST that is x-form-encoded, it will also be in query string form. All the browser manufacturers have standardized around this approach. By default, forms in HTML will send data to the server in this way also.

The querystring module is also used as a helper module to the URL module. Specifically, when decoding URLs, you can ask URL to turn the query string into an object for you rather than just a string. That's described in more detail in the previous section, but the parsing that is done uses the parse method from querystring.

Another important part of querystring is encode (Example 4-15). This function takes a query string's key-value pair object and stringifies it. This is really useful when you're working with HTTP requests, especially POST data. It makes it easy to work with a Java-Script object until you need to send the data over the wire and then simply encode it at that point. Any JavaScript object can be used, but ideally you should use an object that has only the data that you want in it because the encode method will add all properties of the object. However, if the property value isn't a string, Boolean, or number, it won't be serialized and the key will just be included with an empty value.

Example 4-15. Encoding an object into a query string

```
> var myObj = {'a':1, 'b':5, 'c':'cats', 'func': function(){console.log('dogs')}}
> qs.encode(myObj);
'a=1&b=5&c=cats&func='
>
```

I/O

I/O is one of the core pieces that makes Node different from other frameworks. This section explores the APIs that provide nonblocking I/O in Node.

Streams

Many components in Node provide continuous output or can process continuous input. To make these components act in a consistent way, the stream API provides an abstract interface for them. This API provides common methods and properties that are available in specific implementations of streams. Streams can be readable, writable, or both. All streams are EventEmitter instances, allowing them to emit events.

Readable streams

The readable stream API is a set of methods and events that provides access to chunks of data as they are sent by an underlying data source. Fundamentally, readable streams are about emitting data events. These events represent the stream of data as a stream of events. To make this manageable, streams have a number of features that allow you to configure how much data you get and how fast.

The basic stream in Example 4-16 simply reads data from a file in chunks. Every time a new chunk is made available, it is exposed to a callback in the variable called `data`. In this example, we simply log the data to the console. However, in real use cases, you might either stream the data somewhere else or spool it into bigger pieces before you work on it. In essence, the `data` event simply provides access to the data, and you have to figure out what to do with each chunk.

Example 4-16. Creating a readable file stream

```
var fs = require('fs');
var filehandle = fs.readFile('data.txt', function(err, data) {
  console.log(data)
});
```

Let's look in more detail at one of the common patterns used in dealing with streams. The *spooling pattern* is used when we need an entire resource available before we deal with it. We know it's important not to block the event loop for Node to perform well, so even though we don't want to perform the next action on this data until we've received all of it, we don't want to block the event loop. In this scenario (Example 4-17), we use a stream to *get* the data, but *use* the data only when enough is available. Typically this means when the stream ends, but it could be another event or condition.

Example 4-17. Using the spooling pattern to read a complete stream

```
          //abstract stream
var spool = "";
stream.on('data', function(data) {
  spool += data;
});
stream.on('end', function() {
  console.log(spool);
});
```

Filesystem

The filesystem module is obviously very helpful because you need it in order to access files on disk. It closely mimics the POSIX style of file I/O. It is a somewhat unique module in that all of the methods have both asynchronous and synchronous versions. However, we strongly recommend that you use the asynchronous methods, unless you are building command-line scripts with Node. Even then, it is often much better to use the async versions, even though doing so adds a little extra code, so that you can access multiple files in parallel and reduce the running time of your script.

The main issue that people face while dealing with asynchronous calls is ordering, and this is especially true with file I/O. It's common to want to do a number of moves, renames, copies, reads, or writes at one time. However, if one of the operations depends on another, this can create issues because return order is not guaranteed. This means that the first operation in the code could happen after the second operation in the code. Patterns exist to make ordering easy. We talked about them in detail in Chapter 3, but we'll provide a recap here.

Consider the case of reading and then deleting a file (Example 4-18). If the delete (unlink) happens before the read, it will be impossible to read the contents of the file.

Example 4-18. Reading and deleting a file asynchronously—but all wrong

```
var fs = require('fs');

fs.readFile('warandpeace.txt', function(e, data) {
  console.log('War and Peace: ' + data);
});

fs.unlink('warandpeace.txt');
```

Notice that we are using the asynchronous methods, and although we have created callbacks, we haven't written any code that defines in which order they get called. This often becomes a problem for programmers who are not used to programming in event loops. This code looks OK on the surface and sometimes it will work at runtime, but sometimes it won't. Instead, we need to use a pattern in which we specify the ordering we want for the calls. There are a few approaches. One common approach is to use nested callbacks. In Example 4-19, the asynchronous call to delete the file is nested within the callback to the asynchronous function that reads the file.

Example 4-19. Reading and deleting a file asynchronously using nested callbacks

```
var fs = require('fs');

fs.readFile('warandpeace.txt', function(e, data) {
  console.log('War and Peace: ' + data);
  fs.unlink('warandpeace.txt');
});
```

This approach is often very effective for discrete sets of operations. In our example with just two operations, it's easy to read and understand, but this pattern can potentially get out of control.

Buffers

Although Node is JavaScript, it is JavaScript out of its usual environment. For instance, the browser requires JavaScript to perform many functions, but manipulating binary data is rarely one of them. Although JavaScript does support bitwise operations, it doesn't have a native representation of binary data. This is especially troublesome when you also consider the limitations of the number type system in JavaScript, which might otherwise lend itself to binary representation. Node introduces the Buffer class to make up for this shortfall when you're working with binary data.

Buffers are an extension to the V8 engine, which means that they have their own set of pitfalls. Buffers are actually a direct allocation of memory, which may mean a little or a lot, depending on your experience with lower-level computer languages. Unlike the data types in JavaScript, which abstract some of the ugliness of storing data, Buffer provides direct memory access, warts and all. Once a Buffer is created, it is a fixed size. If you want to add more data, you must clone the Buffer into a larger Buffer. Although some of these features may seem frustrating, they allow Buffer to perform at the speed necessary for many data operations on the server. It was a conscious design choice to trade off some programmer convenience for performance.

A quick primer on binary

We thought it was important to include this quick primer on working with binary data for those who haven't done much of it, or as a refresher for those of us who haven't in a long time (which was true for us when we started working with Node). Computers, as almost everyone knows, work by manipulating states of "on" and "off." We call this a *binary state* because there are only two possibilities. Everything in computers is built on top of this, which means that working directly with binary can often be the fastest method on the computer. To do more complex things, we collect "bits" (each representing a single binary state) into groups of eights, often called an *octet* or, more commonly, a *byte*.[3] This allows us to represent bigger numbers than just 0 or 1.

By creating sets of 8 bits, we are able to represent any number from 0 to 255. The rightmost bit represents 1, but then we double the value of the number represented by each bit as we move left. To find out what number it represents, we simply sum the numbers in column headers (Example 4-20).

Example 4-20. Representing 0 through 255 in a byte

```
128 64 32 16 8 4 2 1
--- -- -- -- - - - -
0   0  0  0  0 0 0 0 = 0

128 64 32 16 8 4 2 1
--- -- -- -- - - - -
1   1  1  1  1 1 1 1 = 255

128 64 32 16 8 4 2 1
--- -- -- -- - - - -
1   0  0  1  0 1 0 1 = 149
```

You'll also see the use of hexadecimal notation, or "hex," a lot. Because bytes need to be easily described and a string of eight 0s and 1s isn't very convenient, hex notation has become popular. Binary notation is base 2, in that there are only two possible states

---

3. There is no "standard" size of byte, but the de facto size that virtually everyone uses nowadays is 8 bits. Therefore, octets and bytes are equivalent, and we'll be using the more common term *byte* to mean specifically an octet.

per digit (0 or 1). Hex uses base 16, and each digit in hex can have a value from 0 to F, where the letters A through F (or their lowercase equivalents) stand for 10 through 15, respectively. What's very convenient about hex is that with two digits we can represent a whole byte. The right digit represents 1s, and the left digit represents 16s. If we wanted to represent decimal 149, it is (16 x 9) + (5 x 1), or the hex value 95.

Example 4-21. Representing 0 through 255 with hex notation

```
Hex to Decimal:

0 1 2 3 4 5 6 7 8 9 A  B  C  D  E  F
- - - - - - - - - - -- -- -- -- -- --
0 1 2 3 4 5 6 7 8 9 10 11 12 13 14 15


Counting in hex:

16 1
-- -
0  0 = 0

16 1
-- -
F  F = 255

16 1
-- -
9  5 = 149
```

In JavaScript, you can create a number from a hex value using the notation 0x in front of the hex value. For instance, 0x95 is decimal 149. In Node, you'll commonly see Buffers represented by hex values in console.log() output or Node REPL. Example 4-22 shows how you could store 3-octet values (such as an RGB color value) as a Buffer.

Example 4-22. Creating a 3-byte Buffer from an array of octets

```
> new Buffer([255,0,149]);
<Buffer ff 00 95>
>
```

So how does binary relate to other kinds of data? Well, we've seen how binary can represent numbers. In network protocols, it's common to specify a certain number of bytes to convey some information, using particular bits in fixed places to indicate specific things. For example, in a DNS request, the first two bytes are used as a number for a transaction ID, whereas the next byte is treated as individual bits, each used to indicate whether a specific feature of DNS is being used in this request.

The other extremely common use of binary is to represent strings. The two most common "encoding" formats for strings are ASCII and UTF (typically UTF-8). These encodings define how the bits should be converted into characters. We're not going to go into too much of the gory detail, but essentially, encodings work by having a lookup table that maps the character to a specific number represented in bytes. To convert the encoding, the computer has to simply convert from the number to the character by looking it up in a conversion table.

ASCII characters (some of which are nonvisible "control characters," such as Return) are always exactly 7 bits each, so they can be represented by values from 0 to 127. The eighth bit in a byte is often used to extend the character set to represent various choices of international characters (such as ȳ or ⏹).

UTF is a little more complex. Its character set has a lot more characters, including many international ones. Each character in UTF-8 is represented by at least 1 byte, but sometimes up to 4. Essentially, the first 128 values are good old ASCII, whereas the others are pushed further down in the map and represented by higher numbers. When a less common character is referenced, the first byte uses a number that tells the computer to check out the next byte to find the real address of the character starting on the second sheet of its map. If the character isn't on the second sheet of the map, the second byte tells the computer to look at the third, and so on. This means that in UTF-8, the length of a string measured in characters isn't necessarily the same as its length in bytes, as is always true with ASCII.

Binary and strings

It is important to remember is that once you copy things to a `Buffer`, they will be stored as their binary representations. You can always convert the binary representation in the buffer back into other things, such as strings, later. So a `Buffer` is defined only by its size, not by the encoding or any other indication of its meaning.

Given that `Buffer` is opaque, how big does it need to be in order to store a particular string of input? As we've said, a UTF character can occupy up to 4 bytes, so to be safe, you should define a `Buffer` to be four times the size of the largest input you can accept, measured in UTF characters. There may be ways you can reduce this burden; for instance, if you limit your input to European languages, you'll know there will be at most 2 bytes per character.

Using Buffers

`Buffer`s can be created using three possible parameters: the length of the `Buffer` in bytes, an array of bytes to copy into the `Buffer`, or a string to copy into the `Buffer`. The first and last methods are by far the most common. There aren't too many instances where you are likely to have a JavaScript array of bytes.[4]

---

4. It's very memory-inefficient, for one thing. If you store each byte as a number, for instance, you are using a 64-bit memory space to represent 8 bits.

Creating a `Buffer` of a particular size is a very common scenario and easy to deal with. Simply put, you specify the number of bytes as your argument when creating the `Buffer` (Example 4-23).

Example 4-23. Creating a Buffer using byte length

```
> new Buffer(10);
<Buffer e1 43 17 05 01 00 00 00 41 90>
>
```

As you can see from the previous example, when we create a `Buffer` we get a matching number of bytes. However, because the `Buffer` is just getting an allocation of memory directly, it is *uninitialized* and the contents are left over from whatever happened to occupy them before. This is unlike all the native JavaScript types, which initialize all memory so that when you create a new primitive or object, it doesn't assign whatever was already in the memory space to the primitive or object you just created. Here is a good way to think about it. If you go to a busy cafe and you want a table, the fastest way to get one is to sit down as soon as some other people vacate one. However, although it's fast, you are left with all their dirty dishes and the detritus from their meals. You might prefer to wait for one of the staff to clear the table and wipe it down before you sit. This is a lot like `Buffer`s versus native types. `Buffer`s do very little to make things easy for you, but they do give you direct and fast access to memory. If you want to have a nicely zeroed set of bits, you'll need to do it yourself (or find a helper library).

Creating a `Buffer` using byte length is most common when you are working with things such as network transport protocols that have very specifically defined structures. When you know exactly how big the data is going to be (or you know exactly how big it could be) and you want to allocate and reuse a `Buffer` for performance reasons, this is the way to go.

Probably the most common way to use a `Buffer` is to create it with a string of either ASCII or UTF-8 characters. Although a `Buffer` can hold any data, it is particularly useful for I/O with character data because the constraints we've already seen on `Buffer` can make their operations much faster than operations on regular strings. So when you are building really highly scalable apps, it's often worth using `Buffer`s to hold strings. This is especially true if you are just shunting the strings around the application without modifying them. Therefore, even though strings exist as primitives in JavaScript, it's still very common to keep strings in `Buffer`s in Node.

When we create a `Buffer` with a string, as shown in Example 4-24, it defaults to UTF-8. That is, if you don't specify an encoding, it will be considered a UTF-8 string. That is not to say that `Buffer` pads the string to fit any Unicode character (blindly allocating 4 bytes per character), but rather that it will not truncate characters. In this example, we can see that when taking a string with just lowercase alpha characters, the `Buffer` uses the same byte structure, whatever the encoding, because they all fall in the same range. However, when we have an "é," it's encoded as 2 bytes in the default UTF-8 case or when we specify UTF-8 explicitly. If we specify ASCII, the character is truncated to a single byte.

Example 4-24. Creating Buffers using strings

```
> new Buffer('foobarbaz');
<Buffer 66 6f 6f 62 61 72 62 61 7a>
> new Buffer('foobarbaz', 'ascii');
<Buffer 66 6f 6f 62 61 72 62 61 7a>
> new Buffer('foobarbaz', 'utf8');
<Buffer 66 6f 6f 62 61 72 62 61 7a>
> new Buffer('é');
<Buffer c3 a9>
> new Buffer('é', 'utf8');
<Buffer c3 a9>
> new Buffer('é', 'ascii');
<Buffer e9>
>
```

Working with strings

Node offers a number of operations to simplify working with strings and `Buffers`. First, you don't need to compute the length of a string before creating a `Buffer` to hold it; just assign the string as the argument when creating the `Buffer`. Alternatively, you can use the `Buffer.byteLength()` method. This method takes a string and an encoding and returns the string's length in bytes, rather than in characters as `String.length` does.

You can also write a string to an existing `Buffer`. The `Buffer.write()` method writes a string to a specific index of a `Buffer`. If there is room in the `Buffer` starting from the specified offset, the entire string will be written. Otherwise, characters are truncated from the end of the string to fit the `Buffer`. In either case, `Buffer.write()` will return the number of bytes that were written. In the case of UTF-8 strings, if a whole character can't be written to the `Buffer`, none of the bytes for that character will be written. In Example 4-25, because the `Buffer` is too small for even one non-ASCII character, it ends up empty.

Example 4-25. Buffer.write() and partial characters

```
> var b = new Buffer(1);
> b
<Buffer 00>
> b.write('a');
1
> b
<Buffer 61>
> b.write('é');
0
> b
<Buffer 61>
>
```

In a single-byte `Buffer`, it's possible to write an "a" character, and doing so returns 1, indicating that 1 byte was written. However, trying to write a "é" character fails because it requires 2 bytes, and the method returns 0 because nothing was written.

There is a little more complexity to `Buffer.write()`, though. If possible, when writing UTF-8, `Buffer.write()` will terminate the character string with a NUL character.[5] This is much more significant when writing into the middle of a larger `Buffer`.

In Example 4-26, after creating a `Buffer` that is 5 bytes long (which could have been done directly using the string), we write the character f to the entire `Buffer`. f is the character code 0x66 (102 in decimal). This makes it easy to see what happens when we write the characters "ab" to the `Buffer` starting with an offset of 1. The zeroth character is left as f. At positions 1 and 2, the characters themselves are written, 61 followed by 62. Then `Buffer.write()` inserts a terminator, in this case a null character of 0x00.

Example 4-26. Writing a string into a Buffer including a terminator

```
> var b = new Buffer(5);
> b.write('fffff');
5
> b
<Buffer 66 66 66 66 66>
> b.write('ab', 1);
2
> b
<Buffer 66 61 62 00 66>
>
```

console.log

Borrowed from the Firebug debugger in Firefox, the simple `console.log` command allows you to easily output to stdout without using any modules (Example 4-27). It also offers some pretty-printing functionality to help enumerate objects.

Example 4-27. Outputting with console.log

```
> foo = {};
{}
> foo.bar = function() {1+1};
[Function]
> console.log(foo);
{ bar: [Function] }
>
```

---

5. This generally just means a binary 0.

## CHAPTER 5

Helper APIs

This chapter covers a number of APIs that you'll almost certainly use regularly but aren't used as much as those discussed in Chapter 4.

DNS

Programmers, like end users, normally want to refer to things by their domain names instead of their IP addresses. The DNS module provides this lookup facility to you, but it is also used under the hood whenever you are able to use a domain name—for example, in HTTP clients.

The dns module consists of two main methods and a number of convenience methods. The two main methods are resolve(), which turns a domain name into a DNS record, and reverse(), which turns an IP address into a domain. All of the other methods in the dns module are more specialized forms of these methods.

dns.resolve() takes three arguments:

A string containing the domain to be resolved
   This can include subdomains, such as www.yahoo.com. The www is technically a hostname, but the system will resolve it for you.

A string containing the types of records being requested
   This requires a little more understanding of DNS. Most people are familiar with the "address" or A record type. This type of record maps an IPv4 domain to a domain name (as defined in the previous item). The "canonical name," or CNAME, records allow you to create an alias of an A record or another CNAME. For example, www.example.com might be a CNAME of the A record at example.com. MX records point to the mail server for a domain for the use of SMTP. When you email person@domain.com, the MX record for domain.com tells your email server where to send their mail. Text records, or TXT, are notes attached to a domain. They have been used for all kinds of functions. The final type supported by this library is

service, or SRV, records, which provide information on the services available at a particular domain.

A callback
This returns the response from the DNS server. The prototype will be shown in Example 5-2.

As shown in Example 5-1, calling `dns.resolve()` is easy, although the callback may be slightly different from other callbacks you've used so far.

Example 5-1. Calling dns.resolve( )

```
dns.resolve('yahoo.com', 'A', function(e,r) {
  if (e) {
    console.log(e);
  }
  console.log(r);
} );
```

We called `dns.resolve()` with the domain and a record type of A, along with a trivial callback that prints results. The first argument of the callback is an error object. If an error occurs, the object will be non-null, and we can consult it to see what went wrong. The second argument is a list of the records returned by the query.

There are convenience methods for all the types of records listed earlier. For example, rather than calling `resolve('example.com', 'MX', callback)`, you can call `resol veMx('example.com', callback)` instead (see Example 5-2). The API also provides `resolve4()` and `resolve6()` methods, which resolve IPv4 and IPv6 address records, respectively.

Example 5-2. Using resolve( ) versus resolveMx( )

```
var dns = require('dns');

dns.resolve('example.com', 'MX', function(e, r) {
  if (e) {
    console.log(e);
  }
  console.log(r);
});

dns.resolveMx('example.com', function(e, r) {
  if (e) {
    console.log(e);
  }
  console.log(r);
});
```

Because `resolve()` usually returns a list containing many IP addresses, there is also a convenience method called `dns.lookup()` that returns just one IP address from an A record query (see Example 5-3). The method takes a domain, an IP family (4 or 6), and a callback. However, unlike `.dns.resolve()`, it always returns a single address. If you don't pass an address, it defaults to the network interface's current setting.

Example 5-3. Looking up a single A record with lookup( )

```
var dns = require('dns');

dns.lookup('google.com', 4, function(e, a) {
  console.log(a);
});
```

Crypto

Cryptography is used in lots of places for a variety of tasks. Node uses the OpenSSL library as the basis of its cryptography. This is because OpenSSL is already a well-tested, hardened implementation of cryptographic algorithms. But you have to compile Node with OpenSSL support in order to use the methods in this section.

The cryptograph module enables a number of different tasks. First, it powers the SSL/TLS parts of Node. Second, it contains hashing algorithms such as MD5 or SHA-1 that you might want to use in your application. Third, it allows you to use HMAC.[1] There are some encryption methods to cipher the data with to ensure it is encrypted. Finally, HMAC contains other public key cryptographic functions to sign data and verify signatures.

Each of the functions that cryptography does is contained within a class (or classes), which we'll look at in the following sections.

Hashing

Hashes are used for a few important functions, such as obfuscating data in a way that allows it to be validated or providing a small checksum for a much larger piece of data. To use hashes in Node, you should create a `Hash` object using the factory method `crypto.createHash()`. This returns a new `Hash` instance using a specified hashing algorithm. Most popular algorithms are available. The exact ones depend on your version of OpenSSL, but common ones are:

- `md5`
- `sha1`
- `sha256`
- `sha512`
- `ripemd160`

---

1. Hash-based Message Authentication Code (HMAC) is a cryptographic way of verifying data. It is often used like hashing algorithms to verify that two pieces of data match, but it also verifies that the data hasn't been tampered with.

These algorithms all have different advantages and disadvantages. MD5, for example, is used in many applications but has a number of known flaws, including collision issues.[2] Depending on your application, you can pick either a widely deployed algorithm such as MD5 or (preferably) the newer SHA1, or a less universal but more hardened algorithm such as RIPEMD, SHA256, or SHA512.

Once you have data in the hash, you can use it to create a digest by calling *hash*.update() with the hash data (Example 5-4). You can keep updating a Hash with more data until you want to output it; the data you add to the hash is simply concatenated to the data passed in previous calls. To output the hash, call the *hash*.digest() method. This will output the digest of the data that was input into the hash with *hash*.update(). No more data can be added after you call *hash*.digest().

Example 5-4. Creating a digest using Hash

```
> var crypto = require('crypto');
> var md5 = crypto.createHash('md5');
> md5.update('foo');
{}
> md5.digest();
'¬½\u0018ÜLÂø\\íïeOÏÄ¤Ø'
>
```

Notice that the output of the digest is a bit weird. That's because it's the binary representation. More commonly, a digest is printed in hex. We can do that by adding 'hex' as a parameter to *hash*.digest, as in Example 5-5.

Example 5-5. The lifespan of hashes and getting hex output

```
> var md5 = crypto.createHash('md5');
> md5.update('foo');
{}
> md5.digest();
'¬½\u0018ÜLÂø\\íïeOÏÄ¤Ø'
> md5.digest('hex');
Error: Not initialized
    at [object Context]:1:5
    at Interface.<anonymous> (repl.js:147:22)
    at Interface.emit (events.js:42:17)
    at Interface._onLine (readline.js:132:10)
    at Interface._line (readline.js:387:8)
    at Interface._ttyWrite (readline.js:564:14)
    at ReadStream.<anonymous> (readline.js:52:12)
    at ReadStream.emit (events.js:59:20)
    at ReadStream._emitKey (tty_posix.js:280:10)
    at ReadStream.onData (tty_posix.js:43:12)
> var md5 = crypto.createHash('md5');
> md5.update('foo');
```

2. It's possible to deliberately make two pieces of data with the same MD5 checksum, which for some purposes can make the algorithm less desirable. More modern algorithms are less prone to this, although people are finding similar problems with SHA1 now.

```
{}
> md5.digest('hex');
'acbd18db4cc2f85cedef654fccc4a4d8'
>
```

When we call *hash*.digest() again, we get an error. This is because once *hash*.digest() is called, the Hash object is finalized and cannot be reused. We need to create a new instance of Hash and use that instead. This time we get the hex output that is often more useful. The options for *hash*.digest() output are binary (default), hex, and base64.

Because data in *hash*.update() calls is concatenated, the code samples in Example 5-6 are identical.

Example 5-6. Looking at how hash.update( ) concatenates input

```
> var sha1 = crypto.createHash('sha1');
> sha1.update('foo');
{}
> sha1.update('bar');
{}
> sha1.digest('hex');
'8843d7f92416211de9ebb963ff4ce28125932878'
> var sha1 = crypto.createHash('sha1');
> sha1.update('foobar');
{}
> sha1.digest('hex');
'8843d7f92416211de9ebb963ff4ce28125932878'
>
```

It is also important to know that although *hash*.update() looks a lot like a stream, it isn't really. You can easily hook a stream to *hash*.update(), but you can't use stream.pipe().

HMAC

HMAC combines the hashing algorithms with a cryptographic key in order to stop a number of attacks on the integrity of the signature. This means that HMAC uses both a hashing algorithm (such as the ones discussed in the previous section) and an encryption key. The HMAC API in Node is virtually identical to the Hash API. The only difference is that the creation of an hmac object requires a key as well as a hash algorithm.

crypto.createHmac() returns an instance of Hmac, which offers update() and digest() methods that work identically to the Hash methods we saw in the previous section.

The key required to create an Hmac object is a PEM-encoded key, passed as a string. As shown in Example 5-7, it is easy to create a key on the command line using OpenSSL.

Example 5-7. Creating a PEM-encoded key

```
Enki:~ $ openssl genrsa -out key.pem 1024
Generating RSA private key, 1024 bit long modulus
...++++++
............................++++++
e is 65537 (0x10001)
Enki:~ $
```

This example creates an RSA in PEM format and puts it into a file, in this case called *key.pem*. We also could have called the same functionality directly from Node using the `process` module (discussed later in this chapter) if we omitted the `-out key.pem` option; with this approach, we would get the results on an stdout stream. Instead we are going to import the key from the file and use it to create an `Hmac` object and a digest (Example 5-8).

Example 5-8. Creating an Hmac digest

```
> var crypto = require('crypto');
> var fs = require('fs');
>
> var pem = fs.readFileSync('key.pem');
> var key = pem.toString('ascii');
>
> var hmac = crypto.createHmac('sha1', key);
>
> hmac.update('foo');
{}
> hmac.digest('hex');
'7b058f2f33ca28da3ff3c6506c978825718c7d42'
>
```

This example uses `fs.readFileSync()` because a lot of the time, loading keys will be a server setup task. As such, it's fine to load the keys synchronously (which might slow down server startup time) because you aren't serving clients yet, so blocking the event loop is OK. In general, other than the use of the encryption key, using an `Hmac` example is exactly like using a `Hash`.

Public Key Cryptography

The public key cryptography functions are split into four classes: `Cipher`, `Decipher`, `Sign`, and `Verify`. Like all the other classes in `crypto`, they have factory methods. `Cipher` encrypts data, `Decipher` decrypts data, `Sign` creates a cryptographic signature for data, and `Verify` validates cryptographic signatures.

For the HMAC operations, we used a private key. For the operations in this section, we are going to use both the public and private keys. Public key cryptography has matched sets of keys. One, the private key, is kept by the owner and is used to decrypt and sign data. The other, the public key, is made available to other parties. The public key can be used to encrypt data that only the private key owner can read, or to verify the signature of data signed with the private key.

Let's extract the public key of the private key we generated to do the HMAC digests (Example 5-9). Node expects public keys in certificate format, which requires you to input additional "information." But you can leave all the information blank if you like.

Example 5-9. Extracting a public key certificate from a private key

```
Enki:~ $ openssl req -key key.pem -new -x509 -out cert.pem
You are about to be asked to enter information that will be incorporated
into your certificate request.
What you are about to enter is what is called a Distinguished Name or a DN.
There are quite a few fields but you can leave some blank
For some fields there will be a default value,
If you enter '.', the field will be left blank.
-----
Country Name (2 letter code) [AU]:
State or Province Name (full name) [Some-State]:
Locality Name (eg, city) []:
Organization Name (eg, company) [Internet Widgets Pty Ltd]:
Organizational Unit Name (eg, section) []:
Common Name (eg, YOUR name) []:
Email Address []:
Enki:~ $ ls cert.pem
cert.pem
Enki:~ $
```

We simply ask OpenSSL to read in the private key, and then output the public key into a new file called *cert.pem* in X509 certificate format. All of the operations in `crypto` expect keys in PEM format.

Encrypting with Cipher

The `Cipher` class provides a wrapper for encrypting data using a private key. The factory method to create a cipher takes an algorithm and the private key. The algorithms supported come from those compiled into your OpenSSL implementation:

- `blowfish`
- `aes192`

Many modern cryptographic algorithms use block ciphers. This means that the output is always in standard-size "blocks." The block sizes vary between algorithms: `blowfish`, for example, uses 40-byte blocks. This is significant when you are using the `Cipher` API because the API will always output fixed-size blocks. This helps prevent information from being leaked to an attacker about the data being encrypted or the specific key being used to do the encryption.

Like `Hash` and `Hmac`, the `Cipher` API also uses the `update()` method to input data. However, `update()` works differently when used in a cipher. First, `cipher.update()` returns a block of encrypted data if it can. This is where block size becomes important. If the amount of data in the cipher plus the amount of data passed to `cipher.update()` is enough to create one or more blocks, the encrypted data will be returned. If there isn't enough to form a block, the input will be stored in the cipher. `Cipher` also has a new method, `cipher.final()`, which replaces the `digest()` method. When `cipher.final()` is called, any remaining data in the cipher will be returned encrypted, but with enough padding to make sure the block size is reached (see Example 5-10).

Example 5-10. Ciphers and block size

```
> var crypto = require('crypto');
> var fs = require('fs');
>
> var pem = fs.readFileSync('key.pem');
> var key = pem.toString('ascii');
>
> var cipher = crypto.createCipher('blowfish', key);
>
> cipher.update(new Buffer(4), 'binary', 'hex');
''
> cipher.update(new Buffer(4), 'binary', 'hex');
'ff57e5f742689c85'
> cipher.update(new Buffer(4), 'binary', 'hex');
''
> cipher.final('hex')
'96576b47fe130547'
>
```

To make the example easier to read, we specified the input and output formats. The input and output formats are both optional and will be assumed to be binary unless specified. For this example, we specified a binary input format because we're passing a new `Buffer` (containing whatever random junk was in memory), along with hex output to produce something easier to read. You can see that the first time we call `cipher.update()`, with 4 bytes of data, we get back an empty string. The second time, because we have enough data to generate a block, we get the encrypted data back as hex. When we call `cipher.final()`, there isn't enough data to create a full block, so the output is padded and a full (and final) block is returned. If we sent more data than would fit in a single block, `cipher.final()` would output as many blocks as it could before padding. Because `cipher.final()` is just for outputting existing data, it doesn't accept an input format.

Decrypting with Decipher

The `Decipher` class is almost the exact inverse of the `Cipher` class. You can pass encrypted data to a `Decipher` object using `decipher.update()`, and it will stream the data into blocks until it can output the unencrypted data. You might think that since `cipher.update()` and `cipher.final()` always give fixed-length blocks, you would have to give perfect blocks to `Decipher`, but luckily it will buffer the data. Thus, you can pass it data you got off some other I/O transport, such as the disk or network, even though this might give you block sizes different from those used by the encryption algorithm.

Let's take a look at Example 5-11, which demonstrates encrypting data and then decrypting it.

Example 5-11. Encrypting and decrypting text

```
> var crypto = require('crypto');
> var fs = require('fs');
>
> var pem = fs.readFileSync('key.pem');
> var key = pem.toString('ascii');
>
> var plaintext = new Buffer('abcdefghijklmnopqrstuv');
> var encrypted = "";
> var cipher = crypto.createCipher('blowfish', key);
> ..
> encrypted += cipher.update(plaintext, 'binary', 'hex');
> encrypted += cipher.final('hex');
>
> var decrypted = "";
> var decipher = crypto.createDecipher('blowfish', key);
> decrypted += decipher.update(encrypted, 'hex', 'binary');
> decrypted += decipher.final('binary');
>
> var output = new Buffer(decrypted);
>
> output
<Buffer 61 62 63 64 65 66 67 68 69 6a 6b 6c 6d 6e 6f 70 71 72 73 74 75 76>
> plaintext
<Buffer 61 62 63 64 65 66 67 68 69 6a 6b 6c 6d 6e 6f 70 71 72 73 74 75 76>
>
```

It is important to make sure both the input and output formats match up for both the plain text and the encrypted data. It's also worth noting that in order to get a `Buffer`, you'll have to make one from the strings returned by `Cipher` and `Decipher`.

Creating signatures using Sign

Signatures verify that some data has been authenticated by the signer using the private key. However, unlike with HMAC, the public key can be used to authenticate the signature. The API for `Sign` is nearly identical to that for HMAC (see Example 5-12). `crypto.createSign()` is used to make a `sign` object. `createSign()` takes only the signing algorithm. `sign.update()` allows you to add data to the `sign` object. When you want to create the signature, call `sign.sign()` with a private key to sign the data.

Example 5-12. Signing data with Sign

```
> var sign = crypto.createSign('RSA-SHA256');
> sign.update('abcdef');
{}
> sig = sign.sign(key, 'hex');
'35eb47af5260a00c7bad26edfbe7732a897a3a03290963e3d17f48331a42...aa81b'
>
```

Verifying signatures with Verify

The `Verify` API uses a method like the ones we've just discussed (see Example 5-13), `verify.update()`, to add data—and when you have added all the data to be verified against the signature, `verify.verify()` validates the signature. It takes the `cert` (the public key), the signature, and the format of the signature.

Example 5-13. Verifying signatures

```
> var crypto = require('crypto');
> var fs = require('fs');
>
> var privatePem = fs.readFileSync('key.pem');
> var publicPem = fs.readFileSync('cert.pem');
> var key = privatePem.toString();
> var pubkey = publicPem.toString();
>
> var data = "abcdef"
>
> var sign = crypto.createSign('RSA-SHA256');
> sign.update(data);
{}
> var sig = sign.sign(key, 'hex');
>
> var verify = crypto.createVerify('RSA-SHA256');
> verify.update(data);
{}
> verify.verify(pubkey, sig, 'hex');
1
```

Processes

Although Node abstracts a lot of things from the operating system, you are still running in an operating system and may want to interact more directly with it. Node allows you to interact with system processes that already exist, as well as create new child processes to do work of various kinds. Although Node itself is generally a "fat" thread with a single event loop, you are free to start other processes (threads) to do work outside of the event loop.

process Module

The `process` module enables you to get information about and change the settings of the current Node process. Unlike most modules, the `process` module is global and is always available as the variable `process`.

process events

`process` is an instance of `EventEmitter`, so it provides events based on systems calls to the Node process. The `exit` event provides a final hook before the Node process exits (see Example 5-14). Importantly, the event loop will not run after the `exit` event, so only code without callbacks will be executed.

Example 5-14. Calling code when Node is exiting

```
process.on('exit', function () {
  setTimeout(function () {
   console.log('This will not run');
  }, 100);
  console.log('Bye.');
});
```

Because the loop isn't going to run again, the `setTimeout()` code will never be evaluated.

An extremely useful event provided by `process` is `uncaughtException` (Example 5-15). After you've spent any time with Node, you'll find that exceptions that hit the main event loop will kill your Node process. In many use cases, especially servers that are expected to never be down, this is unacceptable. The `uncaughtException` event provides an extremely brute-force way of catching these exceptions. It's really a last line of defense, but it's extremely useful for that purpose.

Example 5-15. Trapping an exception with the uncaughtException event

```
process.on('uncaughtException', function (err) {
  console.log('Caught exception: ' + err);
});

setTimeout(function () {
  console.log('This will still run.');
}, 500);

// Intentionally cause an exception, but don't catch it.
nonexistentFunc();
console.log('This will not run.');
```

Let's break down what's happening. First, we create an event listener for `uncaught Exception`. This is not a smart handler; it simply outputs the exception to stdout. If this Node script were running as a server, stdout could easily be used to save the log into a file and capture these errors. However, because it captures the event for a nonexistent function, Node will not exit, but the standard flow is still disrupted. We know that all the JavaScript runs once, and then any callbacks will be run each time their event listener emits an event. In this scenario, because `nonexistentFunc()` will throw an exception, no code following it will be called. However, any code that has already been run will continue to run. This means that `setTimeout()` will still call. This is significant when you're writing servers. Let's consider some more code in this area, shown in Example 5-16.

Example 5-16. The effect on callbacks of catching exceptions

```
var http = require('http');
var server = http.createServer(function(req,res) {
  res.writeHead(200, {});
  res.end('response');
  badLoggingCall('sent response');
  console.log('sent response');
});

process.on('uncaughtException', function(e) {
  console.log(e);
});

server.listen(8080);
```

This code creates a simple HTTP server and then listens for any uncaught exceptions at the process level. In our HTTP server, the callback deliberately calls a bad function after we've sent the HTTP response. Example 5-17 shows the console output for this script.

Example 5-17. Output of Example 5-16

```
Enki:~ $ node ex-test.js
{ stack: [Getter/Setter],
  arguments: [ 'badLoggingCall' ],
  type: 'not_defined',
  message: [Getter/Setter] }
{ stack: [Getter/Setter],
  arguments: [ 'badLoggingCall' ],
  type: 'not_defined',
  message: [Getter/Setter] }
{ stack: [Getter/Setter],
  arguments: [ 'badLoggingCall' ],
  type: 'not_defined',
  message: [Getter/Setter] }
{ stack: [Getter/Setter],
  arguments: [ 'badLoggingCall' ],
  type: 'not_defined',
  message: [Getter/Setter] }
```

When we start the example script, the server is available, and we have made a number of HTTP requests to it. Notice that the server doesn't shut down at any point. Instead, the errors are logged using the function attached to the uncaughtException event. However, we are still serving complete HTTP requests. Why? Node deliberately prevented the callback in process from proceeding and calling console.log(). The error affected only the process we spawned and the server kept running, so any other code was unaffected by the exception encapsulated in one specific code path.

It's important to understand the way that listeners are implemented in Node. Let's take a look at Example 5-18.

Example 5-18. The abbreviated listener code for EventEmitter

```
EventEmitter.prototype.emit = function(type) {

...

  var handler = this._events[type];

...

  } else if (isArray(handler)) {
    var args = Array.prototype.slice.call(arguments, 1);

    var listeners = handler.slice();
    for (var i = 0, l = listeners.length; i < l; i++) {
      listeners[i].apply(this, args);
    }
    return true;

...

};
```

After an event is emitted, one of the checks in the runtime handler is to see whether there is an array of listeners. If there is more than one listener, the runtime calls the listeners by looping through the array in order. This means that the first attached listener will be called first with apply(), then the second, and so on. What's important to note here is that *all* listeners on the same event are part of the same code path. So an uncaught exception in one callback will stop execution for all other callbacks on the same event. However, an uncaught exception in one instance of an event won't affect other events.

We also get access to a number of system events through process. When the process gets a signal, it is exposed to Node via events emitted by process. An operating system can generate a lot of POSIX system events, which can be found in the *sigaction(2)* manpage. Really common ones include SIGINT, the interrupt signal. Typically, a SIGINT is what happens when you press Ctrl-C in the terminal on a running process. Unless you handle the signal events via process, Node will just perform the default action; in the case of a SIGINT, the default is to immediately kill the process. You can change default behavior (except for a couple of signals that can never get caught) through the process.on() method (Example 5-19).

Example 5-19. Catching signals to the Node process

```
// Start reading from stdin so we don't exit.
process.stdin.resume();

process.on('SIGINT', function () {
  console.log('Got SIGINT.  Press Control-D to exit.');
});
```

To make sure Node doesn't exit on its own, we read from stdin (described in "Operating system input/output" on page 91) so the Node process continues to run. If you Ctrl-C the program while it's running, the operating system (OS) will send a SIGINT to Node, which will be caught by the SIGINT event handler. Here, instead of exiting, we log to the console instead.

Interacting with the current Node process

Process contains a lot of meta-information about the Node process. This can be very helpful when you need to manage your Node environment from within the process. There are a number of properties that contain immutable (read-only) information about Node, such as:

process.version
> Contains the version number of the instance of Node you are running.

process.installPrefix
> Contains the install path (*/usr/local*, *~/local*, etc.) used during installation.

process.platform
> Lists the platform on which Node is currently running. The output will specify the kernel (linux2, darwin, etc.) rather than "Redhat ES3," "Windows 7," "OSX 10.7," etc.

process.uptime()
> Contains the number of seconds the process has been running.

There are also a number of things that you can get and set about the Node process. When the process runs, it does so with a particular user and group. You can get these and set them with process.getgid(), process.setgid(), process.getuid(), and process.setuid(). These can be very useful for making sure that Node is running in a secure way. It's worth noting that the set methods take either the numerical ID of the group or username or the group/username itself. However, if you pass the group or username, the methods do a blocking lookup to turn the group/username into an ID, which takes a little time.

The process ID, or PID, of the running Node instance is also available as the process .pid property. You can set the title that Node displays to the system using the process.title property. Whatever is set in this property will be displayed in the ps command. This can be extremely useful when you are running multiple Node processes in a production environment. Instead of having a lot of processes called node, or possibly node app.js, you can set names intelligently for easy reference. When one process is hogging CPU or RAM, it's great to have a quick idea of which one is doing so.

Other available information includes process.execPath, which shows the execution path of the current Node binary (e.g., */usr/local/bin/node*). The current working directory (to which all files opened will be relative) is accessible with process.cwd(). The working directory is the directory you were in when Node was started. You can change it using `process.chdir()` (this will throw an exception if the directory is unreadable or doesn't exist). You can also get the memory usage of the current Node process using `process.memoryUsage()`. This returns an object specifying the size of the memory usage in a couple of ways: `rss` shows how much RAM is being used, and `vsize` shows the total memory used, including both RAM and swap. You'll also get some V8 stats: `heapTotal` and `heapUsed` show how much memory V8 has allocated and how much it is actively using.

Operating system input/output

There are a number of places where you can interact with the OS (besides making changes to the Node process in which the program is running) from `process`. One of the main ones is having access to the standard OS I/O streams. stdin is the default input stream to the process, stdout is the process's output stream, and stderr is its error stream. These are exposed with `process.stdin`, `process.stdout`, and `process.stderr`, respectively. `process.stdin` is a readable stream, whereas `process.stdout` and `process.stderr` are writable streams.

process.stdin. stdin is a really useful device for interprocess communication. It's used to facilitate things such as piping in the shell. When we type `cat file.txt | node program.js`, it will be the stdin stream that receives the data from the `cat` command.

Because `process` is always available, the `process.stdin` stream is always initialized in any Node process. But it starts out in a paused state, where Node can write to it but you can't read from it. Before attempting to read from stdin, call its `resume()` method (see Example 5-20). Until then, Node will just fill the read buffer for the stream and then stop until you are ready to deal with it. This approach avoids data loss.

Example 5-20. Writing stdin to stdout

```
process.stdin.resume();
process.stdin.setEncoding('utf8');

process.stdin.on('data', function (chunk) {
  process.stdout.write('data: ' + chunk);
});

process.stdin.on('end', function () {
  process.stdout.write('end');
});
```

We ask `process.stdin` to `resume()`, set the encoding to UTF-8, and then set a listener to push any data sent to `process.stdout`. When the `process.stdin` sends the end event, we pass that on to the `process.stdout` stream. We could also easily do this with the stream `pipe()` method, as in Example 5-21, because stdin and stdout are both real streams.

Example 5-21. Writing stdin to stdout using pipe

```
process.stdin.resume();
process.stdin.pipe(process.stdout);
```

This is the most elegant way of connecting two streams.

process.stderr. stderr is used to output exceptions and problems with program execution. In POSIX systems, because it is a separate stream, output logs and error logs can be easily redirected to different destinations. This can be very desirable, but in Node it comes with a couple of caveats. When you write to stderr, Node guarantees that the write will happen. However, unlike a regular stream, this is done as a blocking call. Typically, calls to Steam.write() return a Boolean value indicating whether Node was able to write to the kernel buffer. With process.stderr this will always be true, but it might take a while to return, unlike the regular write(). Typically, it will be very fast, but the kernel buffer may sometimes be full and hold up your program. This means that it is generally inadvisable to write a lot to stderr in a production system, because it may block real work.

One final thing to note is that process.stderr is always a UTF-8 stream. Any data you write to process.stderr will be interpreted as UTF-8 without you having to set an encoding. Moreover, you are not able to change the encoding here.

Another place where Node programmers often touch the operating system is to retrieve the arguments passed when their program is started. argv is an array containing the command-line arguments, starting with the node command itself (see Examples 5-22 and 5-23).

Example 5-22. A simple script outputting argv

```
console.log(process.argv);
```

Example 5-23. Running Example 5-22

```
Enki:~ $ node argv.js -t 3 -c "abc def" -erf        foo.js
[ 'node',
  '/Users/croucher/argv.js',
  '-t',
  '3',
  '-c',
  'abc def',
  '-erf',
  'foo.js' ]
Enki:~ $
```

There are few things to notice here. First, the process.argv array is simply a split of the command line based on whitespace. If there are many characters of whitespace between two arguments, they count as only a single split. The check for whitespace is written as \s+ in a regular expression (regex). This doesn't count for whitespace in quotes, however. Quotes can be used to keep tokens together. Also, notice how the first file argument is expanded. This means you can pass a relative file argument on the command line, and it will appear as its absolute pathname in `argv`. This is also true for special characters, such as using ~ to refer to the home directory. Only the first argument is expanded this way.

`argv` is extremely helpful for writing command-line scripts, but it's pretty raw. There are a number of community projects that extend its support to help you easily write command-line applications, including support for automatically enabling features, writing inline help systems, and other more advanced features.

Event loop and tickers

If you've done work with JavaScript in browsers, you'll be familiar with `setTime out()`. In Node, we have a much more direct way to access the event loop and defer work that is extremely useful. `process.nextTick()` creates a callback to be executed on the next "tick," or iteration of the event loop. While it is implemented as a queue, it will supersede other events. Let's explore that a little bit in Example 5-24.

Example 5-24. Using process.nextTick( ) to insert callbacks into the event loop

```
> var http = require('http');
> var s = http.createServer(function(req, res) {
... res.writeHead(200, {});
... res.end('foo');
... console.log('http response');
... process.nextTick(function(){console.log('tick')});
... });
> s.listen(8000);
>
> http response
tick
http response
tick
```

This example creates an HTTP server. The `request` event listener on the server creates a callback using `process.nextTick()`. No matter how many requests we make to the HTTP server, the "tick" will always occur on the next pass of the event loop. Unlike other callbacks, `nextTick()` callbacks are not a single event and thus are not subject to the usual callback exception brittleness, as shown in Examples 5-25 and 5-26.

Example 5-25. nextTick( ) continues after other code's exceptions

```
process.on('uncaughtException', function(e) {
  console.log(e);
});

process.nextTick(function() {
  console.log('tick');
});
process.nextTick(function() {
  iAmAMistake();
  console.log('tock');
});
```

```
process.nextTick(function() {
  console.log('tick tock');
});
console.log('End of 1st loop');
```

Example 5-26. Results of Example 5-25

```
Enki:~ $ node process-next-tick.js
End of 1st loop
tick
{ stack: [Getter/Setter],
  arguments: [ 'iAmAMistake' ],
  type: 'not_defined',
  message: [Getter/Setter] }
tick tock
Enki:~ $
```

Despite the deliberate error, unlike other event callbacks on a single event, each of the ticks is isolated. Let's walk through the code. First, we set an exception handler to catch any exceptions. Next, we set a number of callbacks on process.nextTick(). Each of these callbacks outputs to the console; however, the second has a deliberate error. Finally, we log a message to the console. When Node runs the program, it evaluates all the code, which includes outputting 'End of 1st loop'. Then it calls the callbacks on nextTick() in order. First 'tick' is outputted, and then we throw an error. This is because we hit our deliberate mistake on the next tick. The error causes process to emit() an uncaughtException event, which runs our function to output the error to the console. Because we threw an error, 'tock' was not outputted to the console. However, 'tick tock' still is. This is because every time nextTick() is called, each callback is created in isolation. You could consider the execution of events to be emit(), which is called inline in the current pass of event loop; nextTick(), which is called at the beginning of the event loop in preference to other events; and finally, other events in order at the beginning of the event loop.

Child Process

The child_process module allows you to create child processes of your main Node process. Because Node has only one event loop in a single process, sometimes it is helpful to create child processes. For example, you might do this to make use of more cores of your CPU, because a single Node process can use only one of the cores. Or, you could use child_process to launch other programs and let Node interact with them. This is extremely helpful when you're writing command-line scripts.

There are two main methods in child_process. spawn() creates a child process with its own stdin, stdout, and stderr file descriptors. exec() creates a child process and returns the result as a callback when the process is complete. This is an extremely versatile way to create child processes, a way that is still nonblocking but doesn't require you to write extra code in order to steam forward.

All child processes have some common properties. They each contain properties for stdin, stdout, and stderr, which we discussed in "Operating system input/output" on page 91. There is also a `pid` property that contains the OS process ID of the child. Children emit the `exit` event when they exit. Other data events are available via the stream methods of `child_process.stdin`, `child_process.stdout`, and `child_process.stderr`.

child_process.exec( )

Let's start with `exec()` as the most straightforward use case. Using `exec()`, you can create a process that will run some program (possibly another Node program) and then return the results for you in a callback (Example 5-27).

Example 5-27. Calling ls with exec( )

```
var cp = require('child_process');

cp.exec('ls -l', function(e, stdout, stderr) {
  if(!e) {
    console.log(stdout);
    console.log(stderr);
  }
});
```

When you call `exec()`, you can pass a shell command for the new process to run. Note that the entire command is a string. If you need to pass arguments to the shell command, they should be constructed into the string. In the example, we passed `ls` the `-l` argument to get the long form of the output. You can also include complicated shell features, such as | to pipe commands. Node will return the results of the final command in the pipeline.

The callback function receives three arguments: an error object, the result of stdout, and the result of stderr. Notice that just calling `ls` will run it in the current working directory of Node, which you can retrieve by running `process.cwd()`.

It's important to understand the difference between the first and third arguments. The error object returned will be `null` unless an error status code is returned from the child process or there was another exception. When the child process exits, it passes a status up to the parent process. In Unix, for example, this is 0 for success and an 8-bit number greater than 0 for an error. The error object is also used when the command called doesn't meet the constraints that Node places on it. When an error code is returned from the child process, the error object will contain the error code and stderr. However, when a process is successful, there may still be data on stderr.

`exec()` takes an optional second argument with an `options` object. By default, this object contains the properties shown in Example 5-28.

Example 5-28. Default options object for child_process.exec( )

```
var options = { encoding: 'utf8',
                timeout: 0,
                maxBuffer: 200 * 1024,
                killSignal: 'SIGTERM',
                setsid: false,
                cwd: null,
                env: null };
```

The properties are:

encoding
> The encoding for passing characters on the I/O streams.

timeout
> The number of milliseconds the process can run before Node kills it.

killSignal
> The signal to use to terminate the process in case of a time or Buffer size overrun.

maxBuffer
> The maximum number of kilobytes that stdout or stderr each may grow to.

setsid
> Whether to create a new session inside Node for the process.

cwd
> The initial working directory for the process (where null uses Node's current working directory).

env
> The process's environment variables. All environment variables are also inherited from the parent.

Let's set some of the options to put constraints on a process. First, let's try restricting the Buffer size of the response, as demonstrated in Example 5-29.

Example 5-29. Restricting the Buffer size on child_process.exec( ) calls

```
> var child = cp.exec('ls', {maxBuffer:1}, function(e, stdout, stderr) {
... console.log(e);
... }
... );
> { stack: [Getter/Setter],
  arguments: undefined,
  type: undefined,
  message: 'maxBuffer exceeded.' }
```

In this example, you can see that when we set a tiny maxBuffer (just 1 kilobyte), running ls quickly exhausted the available space and threw an error. It's important to check for errors so that you can deal with them in a sensible way. You don't want to cause an actual exception by trying to access resources that are unavailable because you've restricted the child_process. If the child_process returns with an error, its stdin and stdout properties will be unavailable and attempts to access them will throw an exception.

It's also possible to stop a Child after a set amount of time, as shown in Example 5-30.

Example 5-30. Setting a timeout on process.exec( ) calls

```
> var child = cp.exec('for i in {1..100000};do echo $i;done',
... {timeout:500, killSignal:'SIGKILL'},
... function(e, stdout, stderr) {
...    console.log(e);
... });
> { stack: [Getter/Setter], arguments: undefined, type: undefined, message: ... }
```

This example defines a deliberately long-running process (counting from 1 to 100,000 in a shell script), but we also set a short timeout. Notice that we also specified a kill Signal. By default, the kill signal is SIGTERM, but we used SIGKILL to show the feature.[3] When we get the error back, notice there is a killed property that tells us that Node killed the process and that it didn't exit voluntarily. This is also true for the previous example. Because it didn't exit on its own, there isn't a code property or some of the other properties of a system error.

child_process.spawn( )

spawn() is very similar to exec(). However, it is a more general-purpose method that requires you to deal with streams and their callbacks yourself. This makes it a lot more powerful and flexible, but it also means that more code is required to do the kind of one-shot system calls we accomplished with exec(). This means that spawn() is most often used in server contexts to create subcomponents of a server and is the most common way people make Node work with multiple cores on a single machine.

Although it performs the same function as exec(), the API for spawn() is slightly different (see Examples 5-31 and 5-32). The first argument is still the command to start the process with, but unlike exec(), it is not a command string; it's just the executable. The process's arguments are passed in an array as the (optional) second argument to spawn(). It's like an inverse of process.argv: instead of the command being split() across spaces, you provide an array to be join()ed with spaces.

Finally, spawn() also takes an options array as the final argument. Some of these options are the same as exec(), but we'll cover that in more detail shortly.

Example 5-31. Starting child processes using spawn( )

```
var cp = require('child_process');

var cat = cp.spawn('cat');
```

---

3. SIGKILL can be invoked in the shell through kill -9.

```
cat.stdout.on('data', function(d) {
  console.log(d.toString());
});
cat.on('exit', function() {
  console.log('kthxbai');
});

cat.stdin.write('meow');
cat.stdin.end();
```

Example 5-32. Results of previous example

```
Enki:~ $ node cat.js
meow
kthxbai
Enki:~ $
```

In this example, we're using the Unix program cat, which simply echoes back whatever input it gets. You can see that, unlike exec(), we don't issue a callback to spawn() directly. That's because we are expecting to use the Streams provided by the Child class to get and send data. We named the variable with the instance of Child "cat," and so we can access cat.stdout to set events on the stdout stream of the child process. We set a listener on cat.stdout to watch for any data events, and we set a listener on the child itself in order to watch for the exit event. We can send our new child data using stdin by accessing its child.stdin stream. This is just a regular writable stream. However, as a behavior of the cat program, when we close stdin, the process exits. This might not be true for all processes, but it is true for cat, which exists only to echo back data.

The options that can be passed to spawn() aren't exactly the same as exec(). This is because you are expected to manage more things by hand with spawn(). The env, setsid, and cwd properties are all options for spawn(), as are uid and gid, which set the user ID and the group ID, respectively. Like process, setting the uid or the gid to a username or a group name will block briefly while the user or group is looked up. There is one more option for spawn() that doesn't exist for exec(): you can set custom file descriptors that will be given to the new child process. Let's take some time to cover this topic because it's a little complex.

A file descriptor in Unix is a way of keeping track of which programs are doing what with which files. Because Unix lets many programs run at the same time, there needs to be a way to make sure that when they interact with the filesystem they don't accidentally overwrite someone else's changes. The file descriptor table keeps track of all the files that a process wants to access. The kernel might lock a particular file to stop two programs from writing to the file at the same time, as well as other management functions. A process will look at its file descriptor table to find the file descriptor representing a particular file and pass that to the kernel to access the file. The file descriptor is simply an integer.

The important thing is that the name "file descriptor" is a little deceptive because it doesn't represent only pure files; network and other sockets are also allocated file descriptors. Unix has interprocess communications (IPC) sockets that let processes talk to each other. We've been calling them stdin, stdout, and stderr. This is interesting because spawn() lets us specify file descriptors when starting a new child process. This means that instead of the OS assigning a new file descriptor, we can ask child processes to share an existing file descriptor with the parent process. That file descriptor might be a network socket to the Internet or just the parent's stdin, but the point is that we have a powerful way of delegating work to child processes.

How does this work in practice? When passing the options object to spawn(), we can specify customFds to pass our own three file descriptors to the child instead of them creating a stdin, stdout, and stderr file descriptor (Examples 5-33 and 5-34).

Example 5-33. Passing stdin, stdout, and stderr to a child process

```
var cp = require('child_process');

var child = cp.spawn('cat', [], {customFds:[0, 1, 2]});
```

Example 5-34. Running the previous example and piping in data to stdin

```
Enki:~ $ echo "foo"
foo
Enki:~ $ echo "foo" | node

readline.js:80
    tty.setRawMode(true);
        ^
Error: ENOTTY, Inappropriate ioctl for device
    at new Interface (readline.js:80:9)
    at Object.createInterface (readline.js:38:10)
    at new REPLServer (repl.js:102:16)
    at Object.start (repl.js:218:10)
    at Function.runRepl (node.js:365:26)
    at startup (node.js:61:13)
    at node.js:443:3
Enki:~ $ echo "foo" | cat
foo
Enki:~ $ echo "foo" | node fds.js
foo
Enki:~ $
```

The file descriptors 0, 1, and 2 represent stdin, stdout, and stderr, respectively. In this example, we create a child and pass it stdin, stdout, and stderr from the parent Node process. We can test this wiring using the command line. The echo command outputs a string "foo." If we pass that directly to node with a pipe (stdout to stdin), we get an error. We can, however, pass it to the cat command, which echoes it back. Also, if we pipe to the Node process running our script, it echoes back. This is because we've hooked up the stdin, stdout, and stderr of the Node process directly to the cat command in our child process. When the main Node process gets data on stdin, it gets passed to the cat child process, which echoes it back on the shared stdout. One thing to note is that once you wire up the Node process this way, the child process loses its child.stdin, child.stdout, and child.stderr file descriptor references. This is because once you pass the file descriptors to the process, they are duplicated and the kernel handles the data passing. Consequently, Node isn't in between the process and the file descriptors (FDs), so you cannot add events to those streams (see Examples 5-35 and 5-36).

Example 5-35. Trying to access file descriptor streams fails when custom FDs are passed

```
var cp = require('child_process');
var child = cp.spawn('cat', [], {customFds:[0, 1, 2]});
child.stdout.on('data', function(d) {
  console.log('data out');
});
```

Example 5-36. Results of the test

```
Enki:~ $ echo "foo" | node fds.js

node.js:134
        throw e; // process.nextTick error, or 'error' event on first tick
  foo
        ^
TypeError: Cannot call method 'on' of null
    at Object.<anonymous> (/Users/croucher/fds.js:3:14)
    at Module._compile (module.js:404:26)
    at Object..js (module.js:410:10)
    at Module.load (module.js:336:31)
    at Function._load (module.js:297:12)
    at Array.<anonymous> (module.js:423:10)
    at EventEmitter._tickCallback (node.js:126:26)
Enki:~ $
```

When custom file descriptors are specified, the streams are literally set to null and are completely inaccessible from the parent. It is still preferable in many cases, though, because routing through the kernel is much faster than using something like stream.pipe() with Node to connect the streams together. However, stdin, stdout, and stderr aren't the only file descriptors worth connecting to child processes. A very common use case is connecting network sockets to a number of children, which allows for multicore utilization.

Say we are creating a website, a game server, or anything that has to deal with a bunch of traffic. We have this great server that has a bunch of processors, each of which has two or four cores. If we simply started a Node process running our code, we'd have just one core being used. Although CPU isn't always the critical factor for Node, we want to make sure we get as close to the CPU bound as we can. We could start a bunch of Node processes with different ports and load-balance them with Nginx or Apache Traffic Server. However, that's inelegant and requires us to use more software. We could create a Node process that creates a bunch of child processes and routes all the requests to them. This is a bit closer to our optimal solution, but with this approach we just created a single point of failure because only one Node process routes all the traffic. This isn't ideal. This is where passing custom FDs comes into its own. In the same way that we can pass the stdin, stdout, and stderr of a master process, we can create other sockets and pass those in to child processes. However, because we are passing file descriptors instead of messages, the kernel will deal with the routing. This means that although the master Node process is still required, it isn't bearing the load for all the traffic.

Testing Through assert

assert is a core library that provides the basis for testing code. Node's assertions works pretty much like the same feature in other languages and environments: they allow you to make claims about objects and function calls and send out messages when the assertions are violated. These methods are really easy to get started with and provide a great way to unit test your code's features. Node's own tests are written with assert.

Most assert methods come in pairs: one method providing the positive test and the other providing the negative one. For instance, Example 5-37 shows equal() and not Equal(). The methods take two arguments: the first is the expected value, and the second is the actual value.

Example 5-37. Basic assertions

```
> var assert = require('assert');
> assert.equal(1, true, 'Truthy');
> assert.notEqual(1, true, 'Truthy');
AssertionError: Truthy
    at [object Context]:1:8
    at Interface.<anonymous> (repl.js:171:22)
    at Interface.emit (events.js:64:17)
    at Interface._onLine (readline.js:153:10)
    at Interface._line (readline.js:408:8)
    at Interface._ttyWrite (readline.js:585:14)
    at ReadStream.<anonymous> (readline.js:73:12)
    at ReadStream.emit (events.js:81:20)
    at ReadStream._emitKey (tty_posix.js:307:10)
    at ReadStream.onData (tty_posix.js:70:12)
>
```

The most obvious thing here is that when an assert method doesn't pass, it throws an exception. This is a fundamental principle in the test suites. When a test suite runs, it should just run, without throwing an exception. If that is the case, the test is successful.

There are just a few assertions. equal() and notEqual() check for the == equality and != inequality operators. This means they test weakly for *truthy* and *falsy* values, as Crockford termed them. In brief, when tested as a Boolean, falsy values consist of false, 0, empty strings (i.e., ""), null, undefined, and NaN. All other values are truthy. A string such as "false" is truthy. A string containing "0" is also truthy. As such, equal() and notEqual() are fine to compare simple values (strings, numbers, etc.) with each other, but you should be careful checking against Booleans to ensure you got the result you wanted.

The stringEqual() and notStrictEqual() methods test equality with === and !==, which will ensure that only actual values of true and false are treated as true and false, respectively. The ok() method, shown in Example 5-38, is a shorthand for testing whether something is truthy, by comparing the value with true using ==.

Example 5-38. Testing whether something is truthy with assert.ok( )

```
> assert.ok('This is a string', 'Strings that are not empty are truthy');
> assert.ok(0, 'Zero is not truthy');
AssertionError: Zero is not truthy
    at [object Context]:1:8
    at Interface.<anonymous> (repl.js:171:22)
    at Interface.emit (events.js:64:17)
    at Interface._onLine (readline.js:153:10)
    at Interface._line (readline.js:408:8)
    at Interface._ttyWrite (readline.js:585:14)
    at ReadStream.<anonymous> (readline.js:73:12)
    at ReadStream.emit (events.js:81:20)
    at ReadStream._emitKey (tty_posix.js:307:10)
    at ReadStream.onData (tty_posix.js:70:12)
>
```

Often the things you want to compare aren't simple values, but objects. JavaScript doesn't have a way to let objects define equality operators on themselves, and even if it did, people often wouldn't define the operators. So the deepEqual() and notDeep Equal() methods provide a way of deeply comparing object values. Without going into too many of the gory details, these methods perform a few checks. If any check fails, the test throws an exception. The first test checks whether the values simply match with the === operator. Next, the values are checked to see whether they are Buffers and, if so, they are checked for their length, and then checked byte by byte. Next, if the object types don't match with the == operator, they can't be equal. Finally, if the arguments are objects, more extensive tests are done, comparing the prototypes of the two objects and the number of properties, and then recursively performing deepEqual() on each property.

The important point here is that deepEqual() and notDeepEqual() are extremely helpful and thorough, but also potentially expensive. You should try to use them only when needed. Although these methods will attempt to do the most efficient tests first, it can still take a bit longer to find an inequality. If you can provide a more specific reference, such as the property of an object rather than the whole object, you can significantly improve the performance of your tests.

The next assert methods are throws() and doesNotThrow(). These check whether a particular block of code does or doesn't throw an exception. You can check for a specific exception or just whether any exception is thrown. The methods are pretty straightforward, but have a few options that are worth reviewing.

It might be easy to overlook these tests, but handling exceptions is an essential part of writing robust JavaScript code, so you should use the tests to make sure the code you write throws exceptions in all the correct places. Chapter 3 offers more information on how to deal with exceptions well.

To pass blocks of code to throws() and doesNotThrow(), wrap them in functions that take no arguments (see Example 5-39). The exception being tested for is optional. If one isn't passed, throws() will just check whether any exception happened, and does NotThrow() will ensure that an exception hasn't been thrown. If a specific error is passed, throws() will check that the specified exception and only that exception was thrown. If any other exceptions are thrown or the exception isn't thrown, the test will not pass. For doesNotThrow(), when an error is specified, it will continue without error if any exception other than the one specified in the argument is thrown. If an exception matching the specified error is thrown, it will cause the test to fail.

Example 5-39. Using assert.throws( ) and assert.doesNotThrow( ) to check for exception handling

```
> assert.throws(
... function() {
...     throw new Error("Seven Fingers. Ten is too mainstream.");
... });
> assert.doesNotThrow(
... function() {
...     throw new Error("I lived in the ocean way before Nemo");
... });
AssertionError:    "Got unwanted exception (Error).."
    at Object._throws (assert.js:281:5)
    at Object.doesNotThrow (assert.js:299:11)
    at [object Context]:1:8
    at Interface.<anonymous> (repl.js:171:22)
    at Interface.emit (events.js:64:17)
    at Interface._onLine (readline.js:153:10)
    at Interface._line (readline.js:408:8)
    at Interface._ttyWrite (readline.js:585:14)
    at ReadStream.<anonymous> (readline.js:73:12)
    at ReadStream.emit (events.js:81:20)
>
```

There are four ways to specify the type of error to look for or avoid. Pass one of the following:

Comparison function
> The function should take the exception error as its single argument. In the function, compare the exception actually thrown to the one you expect to find out whether there is a match. Return true if there is a match and false otherwise.

Regular expression
> The library will compare the regex to the error message to find a match using the regex.test() method in JavaScript.

String

The library will directly compare the string to the error message.

Object constructor

The library will perform a `typeof` test on the exception. If this test throws an error with the `typeof` constructor, then the exception matches. This can be used to make `throws()` and `doesNotThrow()` very flexible.

VM

The `vm`, or Virtual Machine, module allows you to run arbitrary chunks of code and get a result back. It has a number of features that allow you to change the context in which the code runs. This can be useful to act as a kind of faux sandbox. However, the code is still running in the same Node process, so you should be cautious. `vm` is similar to `eval()`, but offers some more features and a better API for managing code. It doesn't have the ability to interact with the local scope in the way that `eval()` does, however.

There are two ways to run code with `vm`. Running the code "inline" is similar to using `eval()`. The second way is to precompile the code into a `vm.Script` object. Let's have a look at Example 5-40, which demonstrates running code inline using `vm`.

Example 5-40. Using vm to run code

```
> var vm = require('vm');
> vm.runInThisContext("1+1");
2
```

So far, `vm` looks a lot like `eval()`. We pass some code to it, and we get a result back. However, `vm` doesn't interact with local scope in the same way that `eval()` does. Code run with `eval()` will behave as if it were truly inline and replaces the `eval()` method call. But calls to `vm` methods will not interact with the local scope. So `eval()` can change the surrounding context, whereas `vm` cannot, as shown in Example 5-41.

Example 5-41. Accessing the local scope to show the differences between vm and eval( )

```
> var vm = require('vm'),
... e = 0,
... v = 0;
> eval(e=e+1);
1
> e
1
> vm.runInThisContext('v=v+1');
ReferenceError: v is not defined
    at evalmachine.<anonymous>:1:1
    at [object Context]:1:4
    at Interface.<anonymous> (repl.js:171:22)
    at Interface.emit (events.js:64:17)
    at Interface._onLine (readline.js:153:10)
    at Interface._line (readline.js:408:8)
```

```
    at Interface._ttyWrite (readline.js:585:14)
    at ReadStream.<anonymous> (readline.js:73:12)
    at ReadStream.emit (events.js:81:20)
    at ReadStream._emitKey (tty_posix.js:307:10)
>
> vm.runInThisContext('v=0');
0
> vm.runInThisContext('v=v+1');
1
>
0
```

We've created two variables, e and v. When we use the e variable with eval(), the end result of the statement applies back to the main context. However, when we try the same thing with v and vm.runInThisContext(), we get an exception because we refer to v on the right side of the equals sign, and that variable is not defined. Whereas eval() runs in the local scope, vm does not.

The vm subsystem actually maintains its own local context that persists from one invocation of vm to another. Thus, if we create v within the scope of the vm, the variable subsequently is available to later vm invocations, maintaining the state in which the first vm left it. However, the variable from the vm has no impact on v in the local scope of the main event loop.

It's also possible to pass a preexisting context to vm. This context will be used in place of the default context.

Example 5-42 uses vm.runInNewContext(), which takes a context object as a second argument. The scope of that object becomes the context for the code we run with vm. If we continue to pass it from object to object, the context will be modified. However, the context is also available to the global scope.

Example 5-42. Passing a context in to vm

```
> var vm = require('vm');
> var context = { alphabet:"" };
> vm.runInNewContext("alphabet+='a'", context);
'a'
> vm.runInNewContext("alphabet+='b'", context);
'ab'
> context
{ alphabet: 'ab' }
>
```

You can also compile vm.Script objects (Example 5-43). These save a piece of code that you can then run repeatedly. At runtime, you can choose the context to be applied. This is helpful when you are repeatedly running the same code against multiple contexts.

Example 5-43. Compiling code into a script with vm

```
> var vm = require('vm');
> var fs = require('fs');
>
> var code = fs.readFileSync('example.js');
> code.toString();
'console.log(output);\n'
>
> var script = vm.createScript(code);
> script.runInNewContext({output:"Kick Ass"});
ReferenceError: console is not defined
    at undefined:1:1
    at [object Context]:1:8
    at Interface.<anonymous> (repl.js:171:22)
    at Interface.emit (events.js:64:17)
    at Interface._onLine (readline.js:153:10)
    at Interface._line (readline.js:408:8)
    at Interface._ttyWrite (readline.js:585:14)
    at ReadStream.<anonymous> (readline.js:73:12)
    at ReadStream.emit (events.js:81:20)
    at ReadStream._emitKey (tty_posix.js:307:10)
> script.runInNewContext({"console":console,"output":"Kick Ass"});
Kick Ass
```

This example reads in a JavaScript file that contains the simple command con
sole.log(output);. we compile this into a `script` object, which means we can then run
`script.runInNewContext()` on the `script` and pass in a context. We deliberately trig-
gered an error to show that, just as when running vm.runInNewContext(), you need to
pass in the objects to which you refer (such as the `console` object); otherwise, even basic
global functions are not available. It's also worth noting that the exception is thrown
from undefined:1:1.

All the vm run commands take a filename as an optional final argument. It doesn't
change the functionality, but allows you to set the name of the file that appears in a
message when an error is thrown. This is useful if you load a lot of files from disk and
run them because it tells you which piece of code threw an error. The parameter is
totally arbitrary, so you could use whatever string is meaningful to help you debug the
code.

## CHAPTER 6

Data Access

Like any web server, Node needs access to data stores for persistent storage; without persistence, all you have is a brochure website, which would make using Node pointless. In this chapter, we'll run through the basic ways to connect to common open source database choices and to store and retrieve data.

NoSQL and Document Stores

The following NoSQL and document stores are increasingly popular for web-facing applications and are easy to use with Node.

CouchDB

CouchDB provides MVCC-based[1] document storage in a JavaScript environment. When documents (records) are added or updated in CouchDB, the entire dataset is saved to storage and older versions of that data marked obsolete. Older versions of the record can still be merged into the newest version, but in every case a whole new version is created and written to contiguous memory for faster read times. CouchDB is said to be "eventually consistent." In a large, scalable deployment, multiple instances can sometimes serve older, unsynced versions of records to clients with the expectation that any changes to those records will eventually be merged into the master.

Installation

Specific CouchDB libraries are not required to access the database, but they are useful for providing a high level of abstraction and making code easier to work with. A CouchDB server is needed to test any examples, but it does not require a lot of work to get it running.

---

1. MVCC stands for multi-version concurrency control.

Installing CouchDB. The most recent version of CouchDB can be installed from the Apache project page (*http://couchdb.apache.org/downloads.html*). Installation instructions for a wide array of platforms can be found on the wiki (*http://wiki.apache.org/couchdb/Installation*).

If you're running Windows, you will find a number of binary installers as well as instructions for building from source. As with many of the NoSQL options, installation is easiest and best supported on a Linux-based system, but don't be dissuaded.

Installing CouchDB's Node module. Additional modules are not strictly necessary, because CouchDB exposes all of its services through REST, as described in more detail later.

Using CouchDB over HTTP

One of the nice things about CouchDB is that its API is actually all just HTTP. Because Node is great at interacting with HTTP, this means it is really easy to work with CouchDB. Exploiting this fact, it is possible to perform database operations directly without any additional client libraries.

Example 6-1 shows how to generate a list of databases in the current CouchDB installation. In this case, there is no authentication or administrative permission on the CouchDB server—a decidedly bad idea for a database connected to the Internet, but suitable for demonstration purposes.

Example 6-1. Retrieving a list of CouchDB stores via HTTP

```
var http = require('http');

http.createServer(function (req, res) {
  var client = http.createClient(5984, "127.0.0.1");
  var request = client.request("GET", "/_all_dbs");
  request.end();

  request.on("response", function(response) {
    var responseBody = "";

    response.on("data", function(chunk) {
      responseBody += chunk;
    });

    response.on("end", function() {
      res.writeHead(200, {'Content-Type': 'text/plain'});
      res.write(responseBody);
      res.end();
    });
  });
}).listen(8080);
```

A client connection is created with the http library. Nothing distinguishes this connection from any other http connection; because CouchDB is RESTful, no additional communication protocol is needed. Of special note is the request.end() line inside the createServer method. If this line is omitted, the request will hang.

As mentioned earlier, all CouchDB methods are exposed in HTTP calls. Creating and deleting databases, therefore, involves making the appropriate PUT and DELETE statements against the server, as demonstrated in Example 6-2.

Example 6-2. Creating a CouchDB database

```
var client = http.createClient(5984, "127.0.0.1")
var request = client.request("PUT", "/dbname");
request.end();

request.on("response", function(response) {
  response.on("end", function() {
    if ( response.statusCode == 201 ) {
      console.log("Database successfully created.");
    } else {
      console.log("Could not create database.");
    }
  });
});
```

Here, /dbname refers to the resource being accessed. Combined with a PUT command, CouchDB is instructed to create a new database called dbname. An HTTP response code of 201 confirms that the database was created.

As shown in Example 6-3, deleting the resource is the reverse of a PUT: the DELETE command. An HTTP response code of 200 confirms the request was completed successfully.

Example 6-3. Deleting a CouchDB database

```
var client = http.createClient(5984, "127.0.0.1")
var request = client.request("DELETE", "/dbname");
request.end();

request.on("response", function(response) {
  response.on("end", function() {
    if ( response.statusCode == 200 ) {
      console.log("Deleted database.");
    } else {
      console.log("Could not delete database.");
    }
  });
});
```

These elements aren't very useful on their own, but they can be put together to form a very basic (if unfriendly) database manager using the methods shown in Example 6-4.

Example 6-4. A simple CouchDB database creation form

```
var http = require('http');
var qs = require('querystring');
var url = require('url');

var dbHost = "127.0.0.1";
var dbPort = 5984;

deleteDb = function(res, dbpath) {
  var client = http.createClient(dbPort, dbHost)
  var request = client.request("DELETE", dbpath);
  request.end();

  request.on("response", function(response) {
    response.on("end", function() {
      if ( response.statusCode == 200 ) {
        showDbs(res, "Deleted database.");
      } else {
        showDbs(res, "Could not delete database.");
      }
    });
  });
}

createDb = function(res, dbname) {
  var client = http.createClient(dbPort, dbHost)
  var request = client.request("PUT", "/" + dbname);
  request.end();

  request.on("response", function(response) {
    response.on("end", function() {
      if ( response.statusCode == 201 ) {
        showDbs(res, dbname + " created.");
      } else {
        showDbs(res, "Could not create " + dbname);
      }
    });
  });
}

showDbs = function(res, message) {
  var client = http.createClient(dbPort, dbHost);
  var request = client.request("GET", "/_all_dbs");
  request.end();

  request.on("response", function(response) {
    var responseBody = "";

    response.on("data", function(chunk) {
      responseBody += chunk;
    });

    response.on("end", function() {
      res.writeHead(200, {'Content-Type': 'text/html'});
      res.write("<form method='post'>");
```

```
      res.write("New Database Name: <input type='text' name='dbname' />");
      res.write("<input type='submit' />");
      res.write("</form>");
      if ( null != message ) res.write("<h1>" + message + "</h1>");

      res.write("<h1>Active databases:</h1>");
      res.write("<ul>");
      var dblist = JSON.parse(responseBody);
      for ( i = 0; i < dblist.length; i++ ) {
        var dbname = dblist[i];
        res.write("<li><a href='/" + dbname + "'>"+dbname+"</a></li>");
      }
      res.write("</ul>");
      res.end();
    });
  });
};

http.createServer(function (req, res) {
  if ( req.method == 'POST' ) {
    // Parse the request
    var body = '';
    req.on('data', function (data) {
      body += data;
    });
    req.on('end', function () {
      var POST = qs.parse(body);
      var dbname = POST['dbname'];
      if ( null != dbname ) {
        // Create the DB
        createDb(res,dbname);
      } else {
        showDbs(res, "Bad DB name, cannot create database.");
      }
    });
  } else {
    var path = url.parse(req.url).pathname;
    if ( path != "/" ) {
      deleteDb(res,path);
    } else {
      showDbs(res);
    }
  }
}).listen(8080);
```

Using node-couchdb

Knowing how to work with CouchDB over HTTP is useful, but this approach is verbose. Although it has the advantage of not needing external libraries, most developers opt for higher-level abstraction layers, regardless of how simple their database's native driver implementation is. In this section, we look at the node-couchdb package, which simplifies the interface between Node and CouchDB.

You can install the drivers for CouchDB using npm:

```
npm install felix-couchdb
```

Working with databases. The module's first obvious benefit is succinct program code, as demonstrated in Example 6-5.

Example 6-5. Creating a table in CouchDB

```
var dbHost = "127.0.0.1";
var dbPort = 5984;
var dbName = 'users';

var couchdb = require('felix-couchdb');
var client = couchdb.createClient(dbPort, dbHost);
var db = client.db(dbName);

db.exists(function(err, exists) {
  if (!exists) {
    db.create();
    console.log('Database ' + dbName + ' created.');
  } else {
    console.log('Database ' + dbName + ' exists.');
  }
});
```

This example checks for a database called users, creating one if it doesn't already exist. Notice the similarities between the createClient function call here and the one from the http module demonstrated earlier. This is no accident; even though the module makes CouchDB's interfaces easier to work with, in the end you are using HTTP to transmit data.

Creating documents. In Example 6-6, we'll save a document into the CouchDB database created in the previous example.

Example 6-6. Creating a document in CouchDB

```
var dbHost = "127.0.0.1";
var dbPort = 5984;
var dbName = 'users';

var couchdb = require('felix-couchdb');
var client = couchdb.createClient(dbPort, dbHost);

var user = {
  name: {
    first: 'John',
    last: 'Doe'
  }
}

var db = client.db(dbName);
```

```
db.saveDoc('jdoe', user, function(err, doc) {
  if( err) {
    console.log(JSON.stringify(err));
  } else {
    console.log('Saved user.');
  }
});
```

This example creates a user named John Doe in the database with the username *jdoe* as its identity. Notice the user is created as a JSON object and passed directly into the client. No more work is needed to parse the information.

After running this example, the user can be accessed in the web browser at *http:// 127.0.0.1:5984/users/jdoe*.

Reading documents. Once documents are stored in CouchDB, they can be retrieved again as objects, as shown in Example 6-7.

Example 6-7. Retrieving a record from CouchDB

```
var dbHost = "127.0.0.1";
var dbPort = 5984;
var dbName = 'users';

var couchdb = require('felix-couchdb');
var client = couchdb.createClient(dbPort, dbHost);

var db = client.db(dbName);

db.getDoc('jdoe', function(err,doc) {
  console.log(doc);
});
```

The output from this query is:

```
{ _id: 'jdoe',
  _rev: '3-67a7414d073c9ebce3d4af0a0e49691d',
  name: { first: 'John', last: 'Doe' }
}
```

There are three steps happening here:

1. Connect to the database server using `createClient`.
2. Select the document store using the client's `db` command.
3. Get the document using the database's `getDoc` command.

In this case, the record with ID `jdoe`—created in the previous example—is retrieved from the database. If the record did not exist (because it was deleted or not yet inserted), the callback's error parameter would contain data about the error.

Updating documents. Updating documents uses the same `saveDoc` command as creating documents. If CouchDB detects an existing record with the same ID, it will overwrite the old one.

Example 6-8 demonstrates how to update a document after reading it from the data store.

Example 6-8. Updating a record in CouchDB

```
var dbHost = "127.0.0.1";
var dbPort = 5984;
var dbName = 'users';

var couchdb = require('felix-couchdb');
var client = couchdb.createClient(dbPort, dbHost);

var db = client.db(dbName);

db.getDoc('jdoe', function(err,doc) {
  doc.name.first = 'Johnny';
  doc.email = 'jdoe@johndoe.com';

  db.saveDoc('jdoe', doc );

  db.getDoc('jdoe', function(err,revisedUser) {
    console.log(revisedUser);
  });
});
```

The output from this operation is:

```
{ _id: 'jdoe',
  _rev: '7-1fb9a3bb6db27cbbbf1c74b2d601ccaa',
  name: { first: 'Johnny', last: 'Doe' },
  email: 'jdoe@johndoe.com'
}
```

This example reads information about the *jdoe* user from the data store, gives it an email address and a new first name, and saves it back into CouchDB.

Notice that saveDoc and getDoc follow the initial read, instead of putting getDoc inside saveDoc's callback. The CouchDB drivers queue commands and execute them sequentially, so this example will not result in a race condition where the document read completes before the updates are saved.

Deleting documents. To delete a document from CouchDB, you need to supply both an ID and a revision number. Fortunately, this is easy after a read, as shown in Example 6-9.

Example 6-9. Deleting from CouchDB

```
var dbHost = "127.0.0.1";
var dbPort = 5984;
var dbName = 'users';

var couchdb = require('felix-couchdb');
var client = couchdb.createClient(dbPort, dbHost);

var db = client.db(dbName);
```

```
db.getDoc('jdoe', function(err,doc) {
  db.removeDoc(doc._id, doc._rev);
});
```

After connecting to the CouchDB datastore, a `getDoc` command is issued here to get the internal ID (the `_id` field) and revision number (`_rev` field) for that document. Once this information has been obtained, a `removeDoc` command is issued, which sends a `DELETE` request to the database.

Redis

Redis is a memory-centric key-value store with persistence that will feel very familiar if you have experience with key-value caches such as Memcache. Redis is used when performance and scaling are important; in many cases, developers choose to use it as a cache for data retrieved from a relational database such as MySQL, although it is capable of much more.

Beyond its key-value storage capabilities, Redis provides network-accessible shared memory, is a nonblocking event bus, and exposes subscription and publishing capabilities.

Installation

As with many of the rest of the database engines, using Redis requires installing the database application as well as the Node drivers to communicate with it.

Installing Redis. Redis is available in source form (*http://redis.io/download*). There isn't anything to do in the way of configuration; just download and compile per the instructions on the website.

If you are using Windows, you are on your own at the time of this writing because Redis is not supported on Windows. Fortunately, there is a passionate community behind Redis development, and several ports have been made available for both Cygwin and native compilation. The port at *https://github.com/dmajkic/redis* compiles to a native Windows binary using MinGW.

Installing Redis's Node module. The `redis` module is available from GitHub (*https://github.com/mranney/node_redis*), but can be installed using npm:

```
npm install redis
```

Optionally, you may install the mimimalist `hiredis` library along with Node's `redis` module.

Basic usage

Example 6-10 demonstrates a basic set and get operation against Redis by Node.

Example 6-10. A basic get and set operation against Redis

```
var redis = require('redis'),
    client = redis.createClient();

client.on("error", function (err) {
    console.log("Error " + err);
});

console.log("Setting key1");
client.set("key1", "My string!", redis.print);
console.log("Getting key1");
client.get("key1", function (err, reply) {
    console.log("Results for key1:");
    console.log(reply);
    client.end();
});
```

This example begins by creating a connection to the Redis database and setting a callback to handle errors. If you are not running an instance of the Redis server, you will receive an error like this:

```
Error Error: Redis connection to 127.0.0.1:6379 failed - ECONNREFUSED,
Connection refused
```

 Note the lack of callbacks in this example. If you need to perform database reads immediately after writing, it is safer to use a callback, to ensure your code is executed in the correct sequence.

After the connection is opened, the client sets basic data for a string key and hash key, and then reads those values back from the store. Library calls have the same names as basic Redis commands (set, hset, get). Redis treats data coming through the set command as strings, and allows for values up to 512 MB in size.

Hashes

Hashes are objects that contain multiple keys. Example 6-11 sets a single key at a time.

Example 6-11. Setting hash values one key at a time

```
var redis = require('redis'),
    client = redis.createClient();

client.on("error", function (err) {
    console.log("Error " + err);
});

console.log("Setting user hash");
client.hset("user", "username", "johndoe");
client.hset("user", "firstname", "john");
client.hset("user", "lastname", "doe");
```

```
client.hkeys("user", function(err,replies) {
    console.log("Results for user:");
    console.log(replies.length + " replies:");
    replies.forEach(function (reply, i) {
        console.log(i + ": " + reply );
    });
    client.end();
});
```

Example 6-12 shows how to set multiple keys at the same time.

Example 6-12. Setting multiple hash values simultaneously

```
var redis = require('redis'),
    client = redis.createClient();

client.on("error", function (err) {
    console.log("Error " + err);
});

console.log("Setting user hash");
client.hmset("user", "username", "johndoe", "firstname", "john", "lastname", "doe");

client.hkeys("user", function(err,replies) {
    console.log("Results for user:");
    console.log(replies.length + " replies:");
    replies.forEach(function (reply, i) {
        console.log(i + ": " + reply );
    });
    client.end();
});
```

We could accomplish the same thing by providing a more developer-friendly object, rather than breaking it out into a list, as shown in Example 6-13.

Example 6-13. Setting multiple hash values using an object

```
var redis = require('redis'),
    client = redis.createClient();

client.on("error", function (err) {
    console.log("Error " + err);
});

var user = {
    username: 'johndoe',
    firstname: 'John',
    lastname: 'Doe',
    email: 'john@johndoe.com',
    website: 'http://www.johndoe.com'
}

console.log("Setting user hash");
client.hmset("user", user);
```

```
client.hkeys("user", function(err,replies) {
    console.log("Results for user:");
    console.log(replies.length + " replies:");
    replies.forEach(function (reply, i) {
        console.log(i + ": " + reply );
    });
    client.end();
});
```

Instead of manually supplying each field to Redis, you can pass an entire object into hmset, which will parse the fields and send the correct information to Redis.

 Be careful to use hmset and not hset when adding multiple objects. Forgetting that a single object contains multiple values is a common pitfall.

Lists

The list type can be thought of as multiple values inside one key (see Example 6-14). Because it's possible to push content to the beginning or end of a list, these collections are ideal for showing ordered events, such as lists of users who have recently received an honor.

Example 6-14. Using a list in Redis

```
var redis = require('redis'),
    client = redis.createClient();

client.on("error", function (err) {
    console.log("Error " + err);
});

client.lpush("pendingusers", "user1" );
client.lpush("pendingusers", "user2" );
client.lpush("pendingusers", "user3" );
client.lpush("pendingusers", "user4" );

client.rpop("pendingusers", function(err,username) {
  if( !err ) {
    console.log("Processing " + username);
  }
  client.end();
});
```

The output from this example is:

```
Processing user1
```

This example demonstrates a first-in-first-out (FIFO) queue using Redis's list commands. A real-world use for FIFO is in registration systems: the quantity of incoming registration requests is too great to handle in real time, so registration data is hived off to a queue for processing outside the main application. Registrations will be processed in the order they were received, but the primary application is not slowed down by handling the actual record creation and introductory tasks such as welcome emails.

Sets

Sets are used in situations where it is desirable to have lists of nonrepeated items, as in Example 6-15.

Example 6-15. Using Redis's set commands

```
var redis = require('redis'),
    client = redis.createClient();

client.on("error", function (err) {
    console.log("Error " + err);
});

client.sadd( "myteam", "Neil" );
client.sadd( "myteam", "Peter" );
client.sadd( "myteam", "Brian" );
client.sadd( "myteam", "Scott" );
client.sadd( "myteam", "Brian" );

client.smembers( "myteam", function(err, members) {
  console.log( members );
  client.end();
});
```

The output is:

```
    [ 'Brian', 'Scott', 'Neil', 'Peter' ]
```

Even though "Brian" was given to the list twice, he was added only once. In a real-world situation, it would be entirely possible to have two team members named Brian; this highlights the importance of ensuring that your values are unique when they need to be. Otherwise, the set can cause unintended behavior when you expect more elements than are actually present due to the removal of repeated items.

Sorted sets

Like regular sets, sorted sets do not allow duplicate members. Sorted sets add the concept of *weighting*, enabling score-based operations on data such as leaderboards, top scores, and content tables.

The producers of the American weight-loss reality show *The Biggest Loser* are real-world fans of sorted sets. In the 11th season of the series, the contestants were split into three groups based upon their age. On air, they had to perform a crude sorting operation by checking a number printed on everyone's shirts and then line up in ascending order under the hot sun. If one of the contestants had brought her Node- and Redis-equipped laptop to the competition, she might have made a small program to do the work for them, such as the one in Example 6-16.

Example 6-16. Ranking a sorted list using Redis

```
var redis = require('redis'),
    client = redis.createClient();

client.on("error", function (err) {
    console.log("Error " + err);
});

client.zadd( "contestants", 60, "Deborah" );
client.zadd( "contestants", 65, "John" );
client.zadd( "contestants", 26, "Patrick" );
client.zadd( "contestants", 62, "Mike" );
client.zadd( "contestants", 24, "Courtney" );
client.zadd( "contestants", 39, "Jennifer" );
client.zadd( "contestants", 26, "Jessica" );
client.zadd( "contestants", 46, "Joe" );
client.zadd( "contestants", 63, "Bonnie" );
client.zadd( "contestants", 27, "Vinny" );
client.zadd( "contestants", 27, "Ramon" );
client.zadd( "contestants", 51, "Becky" );
client.zadd( "contestants", 41, "Sunny" );
client.zadd( "contestants", 47, "Antone" );
client.zadd( "contestants", 40, "John" );

client.zcard( "contestants", function( err, length ) {
  if( !err ) {
    var contestantCount = length;
    var membersPerTeam = Math.ceil( contestantCount / 3 );
    client.zrange( "contestants", membersPerTeam * 0, membersPerTeam * 1 - 1,
      function(err, values) {
        console.log('Young team: ' + values);
      });
    client.zrange( "contestants", membersPerTeam * 1, membersPerTeam * 2 - 1,
      function(err, values) {
        console.log('Middle team: ' + values);
      });
    client.zrange( "contestants", membersPerTeam * 2, contestantCount,
      function(err, values) {
        console.log('Elder team: ' + values);
        client.end();
      });
  }
});
```

The output is:

```
Young team: Courtney,Jessica,Patrick,Ramon,Vinny
Middle team: Jennifer,John,Sunny,Joe,Antone
Elder team: Becky,Deborah,Mike,Bonnie
```

Adding members to a sorted set follows a pattern similar to the one for adding members to a normal set, with the addition of a rank. This allows for interesting slicing and dicing, as in this example. Knowing that each team consists of similarly aged individuals, getting three teams from a sorted list is a matter of pulling three equal groups straight out of the set. The number of contestants (14) is not perfectly divisible by 3, so the final group has only 4 members.

Subscriptions

Redis supports the publish-subscribe (or pub-sub) messaging pattern, allowing senders (publishers) to issue messages into channels for use by receivers (subscribers) whom they know nothing about (see Example 6-17). Subscribers register their areas of interests (channels), and Redis pushes all relevant messages to them. Publishers do not need to be registered to specific channels, nor do subscribers need to be listening when messages are sent. Redis takes care of the brokering, which allows for a great deal of flexibility, as neither the publisher nor the subscriber needs to be aware of the other.

Example 6-17. Subscribing and publishing with Redis

```
var redis = require("redis"),
    talkativeClient = redis.createClient(),
    pensiveClient = redis.createClient();

pensiveClient.on("subscribe", function (channel, count) {
  talkativeClient.publish( channel, "Welcome to " + channel );
  talkativeClient.publish( channel, "You subscribed to " + count + " channels!" );
});

pensiveClient.on("unsubscribe", function(channel, count) {
  if (count === 0) {
    talkativeClient.end();
    pensiveClient.end();
  }
});

pensiveClient.on("message", function (channel, message) {
  console.log(channel + ': ' + message);
});

pensiveClient.on("ready", function() {
  pensiveClient.subscribe("quiet channel", "peaceful channel", "noisy channel" );
  setTimeout(function() {
    pensiveClient.unsubscribe("quiet channel", "peaceful channel", "noisy channel" );
  }, 1000);
});
```

The output is:

```
quiet channel: Welcome to quiet channel
quiet channel: You subscribed to 1 channels!
peaceful channel: Welcome to peaceful channel
peaceful channel: You subscribed to 2 channels!
noisy channel: Welcome to noisy channel
noisy channel: You subscribed to 3 channels!
```

This example tells the story of two clients. One is quiet and thoughtful, while the other broadcasts inane details about its surroundings to anyone who will listen. The pensive client subscribes to three channels: quiet, peaceful, and noisy. The talkative client responds to each subscription by welcoming the newcomer to the channel and counting the number of active subscriptions.

About one second after subscribing, the pensive client unsubscribes from all three channels. When the unsubscribe command detects no more active subscriptions, both clients end their connection to Redis, and the program execution stops.

Securing Redis

Redis supports password authentication. To add a password, edit Redis's configuration file and include a line for **requirepass**, as shown in Example 6-18.

Example 6-18. Snippet from Redis password configuration

```
################################## SECURITY ###################################

# Require clients to issue AUTH <PASSWORD> before processing any other
# commands.  This might be useful in environments in which you do not trust
# others with access to the host running redis-server.
#
# This should stay commented out for backward compatibility and because most
# people do not need auth (e.g., they run their own servers).
#
requirepass hidengoseke
```

Once Redis is restarted, it will perform commands only for clients who authenticate using "hidengoseke" as their password (Example 6-19).

Example 6-19. Authenticating Redis

```
var redis = require('redis'),
    client = redis.createClient();

client.auth("hidengoseke");
```

The **auth** command must occur before any other queries are issued. The client will store the password and use it on reconnection attempts.

Notice the lack of usernames and multiple passwords. Redis does not include user management functionality, because of the overhead it would incur. Instead, system administrators are expected to secure their servers using other means, such as port-blocking Redis from the outside world so that only internal, trusted users may access it.

Some "dangerous" commands can be renamed or removed entirely. For example, you may never need to use the **CONFIG** command. In that case, you can update the configuration file to either change its name to something obscure, or you can fully disable it to protect against unwanted access; both options are shown in Example 6-20.

Example 6-20. Renaming Redis commands

```
# Change CONFIG command to something obscure
rename-command CONFIG 923jfiosflkja98rufadskjgfwefu89awtsga09nbhsdalkjf3p49

# Clear CONFIG command, so no one can use it
rename-command CONFIG ""
```

MongoDB

Because Mongo supplies a JavaScript environment with BSON object storage (a binary adaption of JSON), reading and writing data from Node is extremely efficient. Mongo stores incoming records in memory, so it is ideal in high-write situations. Each new version adds improved clustering, replication, and sharding.

Because incoming records are stored in memory, inserting data into Mongo is non-blocking, making it ideal for logging operations and telemetry data. Mongo supports JavaScript functions inside queries, making it very powerful in read situations, including MapReduce queries.

Using MongoDB's document-based storage allows you to store child records inside parent records. For example, a blog article and all of its associated comments can be stored inside a single record, allowing for incredibly fast retrieval.

MongoDB native driver

The native MongoDB driver (*https://github.com/christkv/node-mongodb-native*) by Christian Kvaleim provides nonblocking access to MongoDB. Previous versions of the module included a C/C++ BSON parser/serializer, which has been deprecated due to improvements in the JavaScript parser/serializer.

The native MongoDB driver is a good choice when you need precise control over your MongoDB connection.

Installation. To install the driver, run the following command:

```
npm install mongodb
```

 "mongodb" is not to be confused with "mongo," discussed later in this chapter.

Data types. Node's MongoDB driver supports the data types listed in Table 6-1.

Table 6-1. Data types supported for MongoDB

Type	Description	Example
Array	A list of items	cardsInHand: [9,4,3]
Boolean	A true/false condition	hasBeenRead: false

Type	Description	Example
Code	Represents a block of JavaScript code that is runnable inside the database	`new BSON.Code('function quotient( dividend, divisor ) { return divisor == 0 ? 0 : divident / divisor; }');`
Date	Represents the current date and time	`lastUpdated: new Date()`
DBRef	Database reference[a]	`bestFriendId: new BSON.DBRef('users', friendObjectId)`
Integer	An integer (nondecimal) number	`pageViews: 50`
Long	A long integer value	`starsInUniverse = new BSON.Long("100000000000000000000000000");`
Hash	A key-value dictionary	`userName: {'first': 'Sam', 'last': 'Smith'}`
Null	A null value	`bestFriend: null`
Object ID	A 12-byte code used by MongoDB to index objects, represented as 24-digit hexadecimal strings	`myRecordId: new BSON.ObjectId()`
String	A JavaScript string	`fullName: 'Sam Smith'`

[a] Because MongoDB is a nonrelational database, it does not support joins. The data type DBRef is used by client libraries to implement logical relational joins.

Writing records. As mentioned, writing records to a MongoDB collection involves creating a JSON object inside Node and printing it directly into Mongo. Example 6-21 demonstrates building a user object and saving it into MongoDB.

Example 6-21. Connecting to a MongoDB database and writing a record

```
var mongo = require('mongodb');
var host = "localhost";
var port = mongo.Connection.DEFAULT_PORT;
var db = new mongo.Db('node-mongo-examples', new mongo.Server(host, port, {}), {});

db.open(function(err,db) {
  db.collection('users', function(err,collection) {
    collection.insert({username:'Bilbo',firstname:'Shilbo'}, function(err, docs) {
      console.log(docs);
      db.close();
    });
  });
});
```

The output is:

```
[ { username: 'Bilbo',
    firstname: 'Shilbo',
    _id: 4e9cd8204276d9f91a000001 } ]
```

Mongoose

Node has a tremendous base of support for Mongo through its Mongoose library. Compared to the native drivers, Mongoose is an expressive environment that makes models and schemas more intuitive.

Installation. The fastest way to get up and running with Mongoose is by installing it with npm:

```
npm install mongo
```

Alternatively, you can download the most recent version from source and compile it yourself using instructions from the Mongoose project's home page at *http://mongoosejs .com*.

Defining schemas. When you use MongoDB, you don't need to define a data schema as you would with a relational database. Whenever requirements change or you need to store a new piece of information, you just save a new record containing the information you need, and you can query against it immediately. You can transform old data to include default or empty values for the new field, but MongoDB does not require that step.

Even though schemas aren't important to MongoDB, they are useful because they help humans understand the contents of the database and implicit rules for working with domain data. Mongoose is useful because it works using human-readable schemas, providing a clean interface to communicate with the database.

What is a schema? Many programmers tend to think in terms of models that define data structures, but don't think much about the underlying databases those models represent. A table inside an SQL database needs to be created before you can write data to it, and the fields inside that table probably closely match the fields in your model. The schema—that is, the definition of the model inside the database—is created separately from your program; therefore, the schema predates your data.

MongoDB—as well as the other NoSQL datastores—is often said to be schemaless because it doesn't require explicitly defined structure for stored data. In reality, MongoDB does have a schema, but it is defined by the data as it gets stored. You may add a new property to your model months after you begin work on your application, but you don't have to redefine the schema of previously entered information in order to search against the new field.

Example 6-22 illustrates how to define a sample schema for an article database and what information should be stored in each type of model. Once again, Mongo does not enforce schemas, but programmers need to define consistent access patterns in their own programs.

Example 6-22. Defining schemas with Mongoose

```
var mongoose = require('mongoose')

var Schema   = mongoose.Schema,
    ObjectId = Schema.ObjectId

var AuthorSchema = new Schema({
    name: {
        first   : String,
        last    : String,
        full    : String
    },
    contact: {
        email   : String,
        twitter : String,
        google  : String
    },
    photo       : String
});

var CommentSchema = new Schema({
    commenter   : String,
    body        : String,
    posted      : Date
});

var ArticleSchema = new Schema({
    author      : ObjectId,
    title       : String,
    contents    : String,
    published   : Date,
    comments    : [CommentSchema]
});

var Author = mongoose.model('Author', AuthorSchema);
var Article = mongoose.model('Article', ArticleSchema);
```

Manipulating collections. Mongoose allows direct manipulation of object collections, as illustrated in Example 6-23.

Example 6-23. Reading and writing records using Mongoose

```
mongoose.connect('mongodb://localhost:27017/upandrunning', function(err){
  if (err) {
    console.log('Could not connect to mongo');
  }
});

newAuthor.save(function(err) {
  if (err) {
    console.log('Could not save author');
  } else {
    console.log('Author saved');
  }
```

```
});

Author.find(function(err,doc){
  console.log(doc);
});
```

This example saves an author into the database and logs all authors to the screen.

Performance. When you work with Mongoose, you don't need to maintain a connection to MongoDB, because all of your schema definitions and queries are buffered until you connect. This is a big deal, and an important way Mongoose serves Node's methodology. By issuing all of the "live" commands at once against Mongo, you limit the amount of time and the number of callbacks to work with your data and greatly increase the number of operations your application is able to perform.

Relational Databases

There are still many good reasons to use a traditional database with SQL, and Node interfaces with popular open source choices.

MySQL

MySQL has become the workhorse of the open source world for good reason: it provides many of the same capabilities as larger commercial databases for free. In its current form, MySQL is performant and feature-rich.

Using NodeDB

The node-db module provides a native code interface to popular database systems, including MySQL, using a common API that the module exposes to Node. Although node-db supports more than just MySQL, this section focuses on using MySQL in your application code. Since Oracle's purchase of Sun Microsystems, the future of MySQL and its community has come under much speculation. Some groups advocate moving to a drop-in replacement such as MariaDB or switching to a different relational database management system (RDBMS) entirely. Although MySQL isn't going away anytime soon, you need to decide for yourself whether it will be the right choice of software for your work.

Installation. The MySQL client development libraries are a prerequisite for the Node database module. On Ubuntu, you can install the libraries using `apt`:

```
sudo apt-get install libmysqlclient-dev
```

Using `npm`, install a package named `db-mysql`:

```
npm install -g db-mysql
```

To run the examples in this section, you will need to have a database called upand
running with a user *dev* who has the password dev. The following script will create the
database table and basic schema:

```
DROP DATABASE IF EXISTS upandrunning;

CREATE DATABASE upandrunning;

GRANT ALL PRIVILEGES ON upandrunning.* TO 'dev'@'%' IDENTIFIED BY 'dev';

USE upandrunning;

CREATE TABLE users(
    id int auto_increment primary key,
    user_login varchar(25),
    user_nicename varchar(75)
);
```

Selection. Example 6-24 selects all ID and user_name columns from a WordPress user
table.

Example 6-24. Selecting from MySQL

```
var mysql = require( 'db-mysql' );

var connectParams = {
  'hostname': 'localhost',
  'user': 'dev',
  'password': 'dev',
  'database': 'upandrunning'
}

var db = new mysql.Database( connectParams );

db.connect(function(error) {
  if ( error ) return console.log("Failed to connect");

  this.query()
    .select(['id', 'user_login'])
    .from('users')
    .execute(function(error, rows, columns) {
      if ( error ) {
        console.log("Error on query");
      } else {
        console.log(rows);
      }
    });
});
```

As you can probably guess, this executes the equivalent of the SQL command SELECT
id, user_login FROM users. The output is:

```
{ id: 1, user_login: 'mwilson' }
```

Insertion. Inserting data is very similar to selection because commands are chained in the same way. Example 6-25 shows how to generate the equivalent to `INSERT INTO users ( user_login ) VALUES ( 'newbie');`.

Example 6-25. Inserting into MySQL

```
var mysql = require( 'db-mysql' );

var connectParams = {
  'hostname': 'localhost',
  'user': 'dev',
  'password': 'dev',
  'database': 'upandrunning'
}

var db = new mysql.Database( connectParams );

db.connect(function(error) {
  if ( error ) return console.log("Failed to connect");

  this.query()
    .insert('users', ['user_login'], ['newbie'])
    .execute(function(error, rows, columns) {
      if ( error ) {
        console.log("Error on query");
        console.log(error);
      }
      else console.log(rows);
    });
});
```

The output is:

```
{ id: 2, affected: 1, warning: 0 }
```

The `.insert` command takes three parameters:

- The table name
- The column names being inserted
- The values to insert in each column

The database drivers take care of escaping and converting the data types in your column values, so you don't have to worry about SQL injection attacks from code passing through this module.

Updating. Like selection and insertion, updates rely on chained functions to generate equivalent SQL queries. Example 6-26 demonstrates the use of a query parameter to filter the update, rather than performing it across all records in the database table.

Example 6-26. Updating data in MySQL

```
var mysql = require( 'db-mysql' );

var connectParams = {
  'hostname': 'localhost',
  'user': 'dev',
  'password': 'dev',
  'database': 'unandrunning'
}

var db = new mysql.Database( connectParams );

db.connect(function(error) {
  if ( error ) return console.log("Failed to connect");

  this.query()
        .update('users')
        .set({'user_nicename': 'New User' })
        .where('user_login = ?', [ 'newbie' ])
    .execute(function(error, rows, columns) {
      if ( error ) {
        console.log("Error on query");
        console.log(error);
      }
      else console.log(rows);
  });
});
```

The output is:

```
{ id: 0, affected: 1, warning: 0 }
```

Updating a row consists of three parts:

- The `.update` command, which takes the table name (users, in this case) as a parameter
- The `.set` command, which uses a key-value object pair to identify the column names to update and their values
- The `.where` command, which tells MySQL how to filter the rows that will be updated

Deletion. As shown in Example 6-27, deletion is very similar to updates, except that in the case of a delete, there are no columns to update. If no where conditions are specified, all records in the table will be deleted.

Example 6-27. Deleting data in MySQL

```
var mysql = require( 'db-mysql' );

var connectParams = {
  'hostname': 'localhost',
  'user': 'dev',
```

```
  'password': 'dev',
  'database': 'upandrunning'
}

var db = new mysql.Database( connectParams );

db.connect(function(error) {
  if ( error ) return console.log("Failed to connect");

  this.query()
    .delete()
    .from('users')
    .where('user_login = ?', [ 'newbie' ])
    .execute(function(error, rows, columns) {
      if ( error ) {
        console.log("Error on query");
        console.log(error);
      }
      else console.log(rows);
    });
});
```

The output is:

```
{ id: 0, affected: 1, warning: 0 }
```

The .delete command is similar to the .update command, except it does not take any column names or data values. In this example, wildcard parameters are demonstrated in the "where" clause: 'user_login = ?'. The question mark is replaced by the user_login parameter in this code before execution. The second parameter is an array, because if multiple question marks are used, the database driver will take the values in order from this parameter.

Sequelize

Sequelize is an object relational mapper (ORM) that takes much of the repetition out of the tasks performed in the preceding sections. You can use Sequelize to define objects shared between the database and your program, then pass data to and from the database using those objects rather than writing a query for every operation. This becomes a major time-saver when you need to perform maintenance or add a new column, and makes overall data management less error-prone. Sequelize supports installation using npm:

```
npm install sequelize
```

As the database and example user were already created for the examples in the previous section, it's time to create an Author entity inside the database (Example 6-28). Sequelize handles the creation for you, so you don't have to take care of any manual SQL at this point.

Example 6-28. Creating an entity using Sequelize

```
var Sequelize = require('sequelize');

var db = new Sequelize('upandrunning', 'dev', 'dev', {
  host: 'localhost'
});

var Author = db.define('Author', {
  name: Sequelize.STRING,
  biography: Sequelize.TEXT
});

Author.sync().on('success', function() {
  console.log('Author table was created.');
}).on('failure', function(error) {
  console.log('Unable to create author table');
});
```

The output is:

```
Executing: CREATE TABLE IF NOT EXISTS `Authors` (`name` VARCHAR(255), `biography`
TEXT, `id` INT NOT NULL auto_increment , `createdAt` DATETIME NOT NULL, `updatedAt`
DATETIME NOT NULL, PRIMARY KEY (`id`)) ENGINE=InnoDB;
Author table was created.
```

In this example, an `Author` was defined as an entity containing a name field and a biography field. As you can see in the output, Sequelize added an autoincremented primary key column, a `createdAt` column, and an `updatedAt` column. This is typical of many ORM solutions, and provides standard hooks by which Sequelize is able to reference and interact with your data.

Sequelize differs from the other libraries shown in this chapter in that it is based on a listener-driven architecture, rather than the callback-driven architecture used elsewhere. This means that you have to listen for both success and failure events after each operation, rather than having errors and success indicators returned with the operation's results.

Example 6-29 creates two tables with a many-to-many relationship. The order of operation is:

1. Set up the entity schemas.
2. Synchronize the schemas with the actual database.
3. Create and save a `Book` object.
4. Create and save an `Author` object.
5. Establish a relationship between the author and the book.

Example 6-29. Saving records and associations using Sequelize

```javascript
var Sequelize = require('sequelize');

var db = new Sequelize('upandrunning', 'dev', 'dev', {
  host: 'localhost'
});

var Author = db.define('Author', {
  name: Sequelize.STRING,
  biography: Sequelize.TEXT
});

var Book = db.define('Book', {
  name: Sequelize.STRING
});

Author.hasMany(Book);
Book.hasMany(Author);

db.sync().on('success', function() {
  Book.build({
    name: 'Through the Storm'
  }).save().on('success', function(book) {
    console.log('Book saved');
    Author.build({
      name: 'Lynne Spears',
      biography: 'Author and mother of Britney'
    }).save().on('success', function(record) {
      console.log('Author saved.');
      record.setBooks([book]);
      record.save().on('success', function() {
        console.log('Author & Book Relation created');
      });
    });
  }).on('failure', function(error) {
    console.log('Could not save book');
  });
}).on('failure', function(error) {
  console.log('Failed to sync database');
});
```

To ensure that the entities are set up correctly, we do not create the author until after the book is successfully saved into the database. Likewise, the book is not added to the author until after the author has been successfully saved into the database. This ensures that both the author's ID and the book's ID are available for Sequelize to establish the association. The output is:

```
Executing: CREATE TABLE IF NOT EXISTS `AuthorsBooks`
          (`BookId` INT , `AuthorId` INT , `createdAt` DATETIME NOT NULL,
           `updatedAt` DATETIME NOT NULL,
           PRIMARY KEY (`BookId`, `AuthorId`)) ENGINE=InnoDB;
```

```
Executing: CREATE TABLE IF NOT EXISTS `Authors`
            (`name` VARCHAR(255), `biography` TEXT,
            `id` INT NOT NULL auto_increment , `createdAt` DATETIME NOT NULL,
            `updatedAt` DATETIME NOT NULL, PRIMARY KEY (`id`))
            ENGINE=InnoDB;
Executing: CREATE TABLE IF NOT EXISTS `Books`
            (`name` VARCHAR(255), `id` INT NOT NULL auto_increment ,
            `createdAt` DATETIME NOT NULL, `updatedAt` DATETIME NOT NULL,
            PRIMARY KEY (`id`)) ENGINE=InnoDB;
Executing: CREATE TABLE IF NOT EXISTS `AuthorsBooks`
            (`BookId` INT , `AuthorId` INT , `createdAt` DATETIME NOT NULL,
            `updatedAt` DATETIME NOT NULL,
            PRIMARY KEY (`BookId`, `AuthorId`)) ENGINE=InnoDB;
Executing: INSERT INTO `Books` (`name`,`id`,`createdAt`,`updatedAt`)
            VALUES ('Through the Storm',NULL,'2011-12-01 20:51:59',
                    '2011-12-01 20:51:59');
Book saved
Executing: INSERT INTO `Authors` (`name`,`biography`,`id`,`createdAt`,`updatedAt`)
            VALUES ('Lynne Spears','Author and mother of Britney',
                    NULL,'2011-12-01 20:51:59','2011-12-01 20:51:59');
Author saved.
Executing: UPDATE `Authors` SET `name`='Lynne Spears',
            `biography`='Author and mother of Britney',`id`=3,
            `createdAt`='2011-12-01 20:51:59',
            `updatedAt`='2011-12-01 20:51:59' WHERE `id`=3
Author & Book Relation created
Executing: SELECT * FROM `AuthorsBooks` WHERE `AuthorId`=3;
Executing: INSERT INTO `AuthorsBooks` (`AuthorId`,`BookId`,`createdAt`,`updatedAt`)
            VALUES (3,3,'2011-12-01 20:51:59','2011-12-01 20:51:59');
```

PostgreSQL

PostgreSQL is an object-oriented RDBMS originating from the University of California, Berkeley. The project was started by professor and project leader Michael Stonebraker as a successor to his earlier Ingres database system, and from 1985 to 1993 the Postgres team released four versions of the software. By the end of the project, the team was overwhelmed by support and feature requests from its growing number of users. After the Berkeley run, open source developers took over the project, replacing the original QUEL language interpreter with an SQL language interpreter and renaming the project to PostgreSQL. Since the first release of PostgreSQL 6.0 in 1997, the database system has gained a reputation as a feature-rich distribution that is especially friendly to users coming from an Oracle background.

Installation

A production-ready client for PostgreSQL, used by large sites such as Yammer.com, can be downloaded from the npm repository, as shown here:

```
npm install pg
```

pg_config is required. It can be found in the libpq-dev package.

Selection

Example 6-30 assumes you have created a database called upandrunning and granted permission to user *dev* with password dev.

Example 6-30. Selecting data with PostgreSQL

```
var pg = require('pg');

var connectionString = "pg://dev:dev@localhost:5432/upandrunning";
pg.connect(connectionString, function(err, client) {
  if (err) {
    console.log( err );
  } else {
    var sqlStmt = "SELECT username, firstname, lastname FROM users";
    client.query( sqlStmt, null, function(err, result) {
      if ( err ) {
        console.log(err);
      } else {
        console.log(result);
      }
      pg.end();
    });
  }
});
```

The output is:

```
{ rows:
  [ { username: 'bshilbo',
      firstname: 'Bilbo',
      lastname: 'Shilbo' } ] }
```

This is a big difference from the chainable methods used by the MySQL driver. When you're working with PostgreSQL, it will be up to you to write your own SQL queries directly.

As in previous examples, calling the end() function closes the connection and allows Node's event loop to end.

Insertion, updates, and deletion

When typing the SQL queries by hand, as we have seen, you might find it tempting to throw data values directly into the code through string concatenation, but wise programmers seek out methods that protect against SQL injection attacks. The pg library accepts parameterized queries, which should be leveraged everywhere that you use values taken from external sources (such as forms on websites). Example 6-31 demonstrates an insertion, and Examples 6-32 and 6-33 show updates and deletes, respectively.

Example 6-31. Inserting into PostgreSQL

```
var pg = require('pg');

var connectionString = "pg://dev:dev@localhost:5432/upandrunning";
pg.connect(connectionString, function(err, client) {
  if (err) {
    console.log( err );
  } else {
    var sqlStmt   = "INSERT INTO users( username, firstname, lastname ) ";
        sqlStmt   += "VALUES ( $1, $2, $3)";
    var sqlParams = ['jdoe', 'John', 'Doe'];
    var query = client.query( sqlStmt, sqlParams, function(err, result) {
      if ( err ) {
        console.log(err);
      } else {
        console.log(result);
      }
      pg.end();
    });
  }
});
```

The output is:

```
{ rows: [], command: 'INSERT', rowCount: 1, oid: 0 }
```

The query command accepts the SQL statement in the first parameter, and an array of values in the second parameter. Whereas the MySQL driver used question marks for the parameter values, PostgreSQL uses numbered parameters. Numbering the parameters gives you a lot of control over how variables are constructed.

Example 6-32. Updating data in PostgreSQL

```
var pg = require('pg');

var connectionString = "pg://dev:dev@localhost:5432/upandrunning";
pg.connect(connectionString, function(err, client) {
  if (err) {
    console.log( err );
  } else {
    var sqlStmt   = "UPDATE users "
                  + "SET firstname = $1 "
                  + "WHERE username = $2";
    var sqlParams = ['jane', 'jdoe'];
    var query = client.query( sqlStmt, sqlParams, function(err, result) {
      if ( err ) {
        console.log(err);
      } else {
        console.log(result);
      }
      pg.end();
    });
  }
});
```

Example 6-33. Deleting from PostgreSQL

```
var pg = require('pg');

var connectionString = "pg://dev:dev@localhost:5432/upandrunning";
pg.connect(connectionString, function(err, client) {
  if (err) {
    console.log( err );
  } else {
    var sqlStmt    = "DELETE FROM users WHERE username = $1";
    var sqlParams = ['jdoe'];
    var query = client.query( sqlStmt, sqlParams, function(err, result) {
      if ( err ) {
        console.log(err);
      } else {
        console.log(result);
      }
      pg.end();
    });
  }
});
```

Connection Pooling

Production environments are often composed of multiple resources: web servers, caching servers, and database servers. The database is typically hosted on a separate machine from the web server, allowing horizontal growth of the public-facing website without the need for setting up and configuring complex database clusters. Application developers must therefore be aware of the performance implications in accessing resources and how those access costs affect their site's performance.

Connection pooling is an important concept in web development because the performance cost of establishing a database connection is relatively high; creating one or more new connections for every request creates an unnecessary burden on a heavily trafficked site and will contribute to weaker performance. The solution is to maintain database connections inside a cache pool after they are no longer needed, so they can be used immediately by the next incoming request.

Many database drivers provide pooling functionality, but that pattern goes against Node's "one module, one purpose" philosophy. Instead, Node developers should use the generic-pool module in front of their data layer to serve new database connections (see Example 6-34). generic-pool will reuse connections where possible to prevent the overhead of creating new database connections, and the module can be used with any data library.

Example 6-34. Using the connection pool with node-db

```
var mysql = require( 'db-mysql' );
var poolModule = require('generic-pool');
```

```
var connectParams = {
  'hostname': 'localhost',
  'user': 'dev',
  'password': 'dev',
  'database': 'zborowski'
}

var pool = poolModule.Pool({
  name : 'mysql',
  create : function(callback) {
    var db = new mysql.Database( connectParams );
    db.connect(function(error) {
      callback(error, db);
    });
  },
  destroy : function(client) { client.disconnect(); },
  max      : 10,
  idleTimeoutMillis : 3000,
  log : true
});

pool.acquire(function(error, client) {
  if ( error ) return console.log("Failed to connect");

  client.query()
    .select(['id', 'user_login'])
    .from('wp_users')
    .execute(function(error, rows, columns) {
      if ( error ) {
        console.log("Error on query");
      } else {
        console.log(rows);
      }
      pool.release(client);
    });
});
```

The output is:

```
pool mysql - dispense() clients=1 available=0
pool mysql - dispense() - creating obj - count=1
[ { id: 1, user_login: 'mwilson' } ]
pool mysql - timeout: 1319413992199
pool mysql - dispense() clients=0 available=1
pool mysql - availableObjects.length=1
pool mysql - availableObjects.length=1
pool mysql - removeIdle() destroying obj - now:1319413992211 timeout:1319413992199
pool mysql - removeIdle() all objects removed
```

The pool works through the magic of the create and destroy functions. When a consumer attempts to acquire a connection, the pool will call the create function if no connections have already been opened. If the connection sits idle for too long (an interval indicated in milliseconds by the idleTimeoutMillis attribute), it is destroyed and its memory resources freed.

The beauty of Node's pool is that any persistent resource can be represented. Databases are a natural fit, but you can just as easily write commands to maintain connections to an outside session cache, or even to hardware interfaces.

MQ Protocols

We used a mailman analogy earlier to describe Node's event loop. If the mailman were to arrive at a closed gate, he would be unable to deliver his message; but imagine an elderly and kind groundskeeper was in the process of opening the gate so the mailman could pass through. Being elderly and somewhat frail from his years of service, it takes the groundskeeper some time to clear the way—time during which the mailman is unable to deliver any messages.

This situation is a blocking process, but it is not a permanent state. Evenually the groundskeeper will manage to get the gate open, and the mailman will go about his business. Every house the mailman reaches with a similar gate-opening process will slow down the overall route. In the context of a Node application, this type of block will seriously degrade performance.

In the computer realm, similar situations may be caused by sending a user email during a registration process, by lots of math that needs to be done as a result of user input, or by any situation in which the time it takes to complete a task exceeds a user's normally expected wait times. Node's event-driven design handles the majority of these situations for you by using asynchronous functions and callbacks, but when an event is particularly "heavy" to process, it doesn't make sense to process it inside Node. Node should only take care of handling results and fast operations.

By way of example, consider a generic user registration process. When a user registers herself, the application saves a new record in the database, sends an email to that user, and perhaps records some statistics about the registration process, such as the number of steps completed or amount of time taken. It probably doesn't make sense to perform all of those actions right away when the user hits the Submit button on your web page. For one thing, the email process could take several seconds (or if you're unlucky, minutes) to complete, the database call may not need to finish before the user is welcomed, and the statistics are probably separate from your main application flow. In this case, you might choose to generate a message that notifies other parts of your application instead—perhaps running on a different machine entirely—that a user has registered. This is known as a *publish-subscribe pattern.*

Another example: suppose you have a cluster of machines running Node.js. When a new machine is added to the cluster, it issues a message requesting configuration information. A configuration server responds to the message with a list of configuration information the new machine needs to integrate into the cluster. This is known as a *request-reply pattern.*

Message queues allow programmers to publish events and move on, enabling improved performance through parallel processing and higher levels of scalability through inter-process communication channels.

RabbitMQ

RabbitMQ is a message broker that supports the advanced message queueing protocol (AMQP). It is useful in situations where data needs to be communicated between different servers, or between different processes on the same server. Written in Erlang, RabbitMQ is capable of clustering for high availability, and is fairly straightforward to install and begin using.

Installing RabbitMQ

If you're using Linux, RabbitMQ is available in package form for most distributions. Anyone can download the software from *http://www.rabbitmq.com* and compile it from source.

Once RabbitMQ has been installed and is running, use npm to retrieve Node's AMQP drivers:

```
npm install amqp
```

Publish and subscribe

RabbitMQ communicates using the standardized protocol AMQP. AMQP comes from the financial services industry, where reliable messaging is a matter of life or death. It provides a vendor-neutral and abstract specification for generic (not just financial) middleware messaging and is intended to solve the problem of communicating between different types of systems. AMQP is conceptually similar to email: email messages have specifications for headers and format, but their contents can be anything from text to photos and video. Just as two companies don't need to run the same email server software to communicate, AMQP allows messaging between different platforms. For example, a publisher written in PHP can send a message to a consumer written in JavaScript.

Example 6-35 shows the most basic elements of RabbitMQ programming.

Example 6-35. AMQP/RabbitMQ usage

```
var connection = require('amqp').createConnection();

connection.on('ready', function() {
  console.log('Connected to ' + connection.serverProperties.product);
  var e = connection.exchange('up-and-running');

  var q = connection.queue('up-and-running-queue');
```

```
    q.on('queueDeclareOk', function(args) {
      console.log('Queue opened');
      q.bind(e, '#');

      q.on('queueBindOk', function() {
        console.log('Queue bound');

        q.on('basicConsumeOk', function() {
          console.log("Consumer has subscribed, publishing message.");
          e.publish('routingKey', {hello:'world'});
        });
      });

      q.subscribe(function(msg) {
        console.log('Message received:');
        console.log(msg);
        connection.end();
      });
    });
});
```

The output is:

```
Connected to RabbitMQ
Queue opened
Queue bound
Consumer has subscribed, publishing message.
Message received:
{ hello: 'world' }
```

The createConnection command opens a connection to the RabbitMQ message broker, which in this case defaults (as per AMQP) to localhost on port 5672. If necessary, this command can be overloaded; for example:

```
createConnection({host: 'dev.mycompany.com', port: 5555})
```

Next, a queue and exchange are defined. This step is not strictly required, because AMQP brokers are required to provide a default exchange, but by specifying up-and-running as the exchange name, you insulate your application from other exchanges that could be running on the server. An exchange is an entity that receives messages and passes them forward to attached queues.

The queue doesn't do anything by itself; it must be bound to an exchange before it will do anything. The command q.bind(e, '#') instructs AMQP to attach the queue named up-and-running-queue to the exchange named up-and-running, and to listen for all messages passed to the exchange (the '#' parameter). You could easily change the # to some specific key to filter out messages.

Once the queue and exchange have been declared, an event is set up for basicConsume Ok, which is an event generated by the AMQP library when a client subscribes to a queue. When that happens, Node will publish a "hello world" message to the exchange under a filtering key of routingKey. In this example, the filter key doesn't matter, because the queue is bound to all keys (via the bind('#') command), but a central tenet of AMQP is that the publisher is never aware of which subscribers (if any) are connected, so a routing key is supplied in any case.

Finally, the subscribe command is issued. The callback function that is passed as its argument is called every time an eligible message is received by the exchange and passed through to the queue. In this case, the callback causes the program to end, which is good for demonstration purposes, but in "real" applications it's unlikely you would do this. When the subscribe command is successful, AMQP dispatches the basicConsume Ok event, which triggers the publishing of the "hello world" message and subsequently ends the demonstration program.

Work queues

Queues are useful when long-running tasks take longer than is acceptable to the user (such as during a web page load) or when the task would otherwise block the application. Using RabbitMQ, is it possible to split tasks among multiple workers and ensure that tasks are completed even if the first worker that handles them dies mid-process (Example 6-36).

Example 6-36. Publishing long jobs with AMQP

```
var connection = require('amqp').createConnection();
var count = 0;

connection.on('ready', function() {
  console.log('Connected to ' + connection.serverProperties.product);
  var e = connection.exchange('up-and-running');

  var q = connection.queue('up-and-running-queue');

  q.on('queueDeclareOk', function(args) {
    console.log('Queue opened');
    q.bind(e, '#');

    q.on('queueBindOk', function() {
      console.log('Queue bound');

      setInterval(function(){
        console.log('Publishing message #' + ++count);
        e.publish('routingKey', {count:count});
      }, 1000);
    });
  });
});
```

This example is a modified version of the straight publish-subscribe example from the previous section, but it is just a publisher, so the event listener for subscribing is gone. In its place is an interval timer that publishes a message to the queue every 1,000 milliseconds (that is, every second). The message contains a count variable that is incremented during each publish. This code can be used to implement a simple worker application. Example 6-37 shows the corresponding client.

Example 6-37. Processing long jobs with AMQP

```
var connection = require('amqp').createConnection();

function sleep(milliseconds)
{
  var start = new Date().getTime();
  while (new Date().getTime() < start + milliseconds);
}

connection.on('ready', function() {
  console.log('Connected to ' + connection.serverProperties.product);

  var e = connection.exchange('up-and-running');
  var q = connection.queue('up-and-running-queue');

  q.on('queueDeclareOk', function(args) {
  q.bind(e,'#');

  q.subscribe({ack:true},function(msg) {
    console.log('Message received:');
    console.log(msg.count);
    sleep(5000);
    console.log('Processed. Waiting for next message.');
    q.shift();
    });
  });
});
```

The client works by taking a message from the queue, processing it (in this example, sleeping for 5 seconds), and then taking the next message from the queue and repeating. Although there is no "sleep" function in Node, you can fake it with a blocking loop, as done here.

There is a problem. Recall that the publisher posts a message to the queue every second. Because the client takes 5 seconds to process each message, it will very quickly get far behind the publisher. The solution? Open another window and run a second client, and now the messages are processed twice as fast. It's still not quick enough to handle the volume produced by the publisher, but adding more clients can further spread the load and keep the unprocessed messages from falling behind. This setup is referred to as *worker queues*.

Worker queues function by round-robining the message publishing between clients connected to a named queue. The {ack:true} parameter to the subscribe command instructs AMQP to wait for the user to acknowledge that the processing has been completed for a message. The shift method provides that acknowledgment by shifting the message off the queue and removing it from service. This way, if the worker happens to die while processing a message, the RabbitMQ broker will send the message to the next available client. There is no timeout; as long as the client is connected, the message will be removed from play. Only when the client disconnects without acknowledging a message will it be sent to the next client.

A common "gotcha" occurs when developers forget to use the q.shift() command. If you forget it, your program will continue to function as normal, but as soon as your client disconnects, the server will place all of the messages the client processed back onto the queue.

Another side effect is that the memory usage by RabbitMQ will gradually rise. This is because, although the messages are removed from active duty on the queue, they are kept in memory until they are acknowledged and deleted by the client.

## CHAPTER 7

Important External Modules

Although the Node core is extremely useful, many of its abstractions are very low-level. So a lot of development in Node is done using higher abstraction libraries built by the community, similar to how Ruby-based websites use Rails or Sinatra rather than custom-written Ruby code. Although these modules aren't technically Node itself, they are extremely important for getting things done, and many of them are mature projects in themselves. This chapter explores some of the most popular and useful community modules for Node.

Express

Express, an MVC framework for Node, is probably the most widely used Node module. It was inspired by the Sinatra framework for Ruby and enables a lot of features that make it very easy to throw together a website with Node.

A Basic Express App

Express works by defining page handlers for *routes*. The routes can be as simple as a path, or much more complex. The handlers could be as simple as emitting "Hello, world" or as complex as a whole page-rendering system that interacts with a database. You'll need to install Express using npm install express before you can start using it. Example 7-1 shows how to create a simple application with Express.

Example 7-1. Creating a simple Express app

```
var express = require('express');

var app = express.createServer();

app.get('/', function(req, res) {
  res.send('hello world');
});

app.listen(9001);
```

This code is obviously pretty similar to http in terms of creating a server. However, a few things are a lot more straightforward. First, app.get() is creating a response to a specific route—in this case, '/'. Unlike a regular http server, which provides a listener for generic requests, Express offers a listener for specific HTTP verbs. So get() will answer only GET requests, put() will answer only PUT requests, etc. Combine that with the route we specified, and you immediately have some powerful functionality. A typical Express program specifies a series of expressions, and Express matches the route in each incoming request against each expression in turn, executing the code associated with the first expression that matches.

 It is possible to have Express skip over expressions under certain conditions, using the next() function discussed later in this section.

The next thing to notice in the example is how we responded. We still use the response object as in http, but Express has provided a send() method. We didn't need to provide any HTTP headers or call end(). The send() method figures out things such as the HTTP headers that should be sent and includes end() automatically.

The point here is that Express takes the basic structure laid out by http and enriches it significantly with a lot of functionality to create real applications quickly. You shouldn't have to create routing code every time you want to deal with HTTP requests, so Express takes care of that stuff.

Setting Up Routes in Express

Routes are one of the core concepts in Express, and one of the things that make it really useful. As mentioned in the previous section, routes are applied to an HTTP verb via a method with the same name, such as get() or post(). The routes consist of a simple string or a regex and can contain variable declarations, wildcards, and optional key flags. Let's take a look at some examples, starting with Example 7-2.

Example 7-2. Route with variable and optional flag

```
var express = require('express');
var app = express.createServer();

app.get('/:id?', function(req, res) {
  if(req.params.id) {
    res.send(req.params.id);
  } else {
    res.send('oh hai');
  }
});

app.listen(9001);
```

This example shows a route that includes an optional variable called `id`. The variable name does not have any special meaning to Express, but it will be available to use inside the callback function. In Express routes, you use a preceding colon (:) to mark a variable you want preserved. The string passed in the URL will be captured into the variable. All routes in Express are actually turned into regular expressions (more on this later) and tokenized[1] for use by application code.[2] The regex used will match up to the next known token in your route. Notice that this variable is also optional. If you run this program and go to *http://localhost:9001*, you'll just get "oh hai" back because you did not put a slash after the port, and the variable part of the route was optional. If you append anything else (so long as you don't include another /), you'll get it back as your response body; matching the `id` token, it will be stored in `req.params.id`.

Express routes will always treat / as a token, but they will also treat it as optional if it terminates the request. So our route `/:id?` will match `localhost`, `localhost/ localhost/ tom`, and `localhost/tom/`, but *not* `localhost/tom/tom`.

Routes can also use wildcards, as shown in Example 7-3. (*) will match anything except the token following it (nongreedy regex matching).

Example 7-3. Using wildcards in routes

```
app.get('/a*', function(req,res) {
  res.send('a');
  //matches /afoo /a.bar /a/qux etc.
});

app.get('/b*/c*d', function(req,res) {
  res.send('b');
  //matches /b/cd /b/cfood /b//c/d/ etc.
  //does not match /b/c/d/foo
});

app.get('*', function(req, res) {
  res.send('*');
  //matches /a /c /b/cd /b/c/d /b/c/d/foo
  //does not match /afoo /bfoo/cbard
});
```

When you use a wildcard to make routes, any tokens between the wildcards must match, unless they are optional. Wildcards are often used for things such as filenames containing periods (.). It's also important to notice that unlike in many regular expression languages, * does not mean zero or more characters; it means one or more characters. A forward slash (/) can be considered a character when matching with wildcards.

---

1. *Tokenized* refers to the process of breaking apart a string of text into chunks (or words) called tokens.

2. This functionality is actually part of a submodule of Express called **router**. You can look at the source code of **router** to see the details of routing regexes.

Another important thing to note is that routes are ordered. Multiple routes can match a given URL, but only the first one that matches will trigger the associated activity. This means that the order in which routes are defined is very significant. In the previous example, the general wildcard will catch everything that wasn't already caught by a previous route, even though it matches all of them.

You can also use regexes to define routes (Example 7-4). If you do this, `router` won't process the regex any further. Because you still might want to get variables out of the URL, you can use captures to define them.

Example 7-4. Using a regex to define a route

```
var express = require('express');
var app = express.createServer();

app.get(/\/(\d+)/, function(req, res) {
  res.send(req.params[0]);
});

app.listen(9001);
```

In this example, the regex will match only URLs that start with a number (\d matches any digit, and the + allows one or more to match). This means that / will not match, but /12 will. However, the regex checking uses `RegExp.match()`, which finds a regex inside a larger string. This means that /12abc will also match. If you want to make sure that a regex represents the complete route, use the $ token at the end of the regex, such as /\/(\d+)$/. $ checks for the end of the line, so the regex will match only if it terminates. You probably want to keep the default Express behavior of loosely matching a / at the end of URLs, though. Do this with \/?$ instead of just $, to allow an optional / at the end of the string.

Notice how we accessed the capture in our regex in Example 7-4. If you use a regex for your route, you can use `req.params` as an array to access the captures as variables. This also works when `router` converts your route to a regex, but you probably want to use the variable names in that case, as we showed earlier. You can also use regex to make better-named variables in routes by constraining what will match that variable, as in Example 7-5.

Example 7-5. Use regex to be more specific about variable types

```
var express = require('express');
var app = express.createServer();

app.get('/:id(\\d+)', function(req, res) {
  res.send(req.params[0]);
});

app.listen(9001);
```

This example constrains the id parameter to numbers by asking `route` to match only numbers with the regex \d+. The capture will still be exposed as `req.params.id`, but it will match only if the regex matched. Because the regex is highly flexible, you can use this technique to capture or restrict URL matching to pretty much anything while still getting named variables to use. Remember to escape any backslash (\) you use in Java-Script strings. (This was not necessary in Example 7-4, because it used a regular expression directly rather than inside a string.)

Sometimes there are multiple routes that match a URL that you want to use in various circumstances. We've already seen that the order in which routes are defined is significant in determining which will be selected. However, it is possible to pass control back to the next route if some criteria isn't met (Example 7-6). This is a great option for a number of scenarios.

Example 7-6. Passing control to another route

```
app.get('/users/:id', function(req, res, next){
  var id = req.params.id;

  if (checkPermission(id)) {
    // show private page
  } else {
    next();
  }
});

app.get('/users/:id', function(req, res){
  // show public user page
});
```

We've added another argument to the function that handles the routes. The `next` argument tells the `router` middleware (we'll discuss middleware shortly in more depth) to call the next route. The argument is always passed to the callback, but this example is the first where we choose to name and use it. In this case, we can check the `id` to see whether the user has permission to view the private version of this page, and if not, send her to the next route, which has the public version.

This combines really well with `app.all()`, the method that describes all HTTP verbs. As Example 7-7 demonstrates, we can capture across a range of HTTP verbs and routes, apply some logic, and then pass control onto more specific routes.

Example 7-7. Using app.all( ) to select multiple HTTP verbs and routes and then pass control back

```
var express = require('express');

var app = express.createServer();

var users = [{ name: 'tj' }, { name: tom }];

app.all('/user/:id/:op?', function(req, res, next){
  req.user = users[req.params.id];
```

```
  if (req.user) {
    next();
  } else {
    next(new Error('Cannot find user with ID: ' + req.params.id));
  }
});

app.get('/user/:id', function(req, res){
  res.send('Viewing ' + req.user.name);
});

app.get('/user/:id/edit', function(req, res){
  res.send('Editing ' + req.user.name);
});

app.put('/user/:id', function(req, res){
  res.send('Updating ' + req.user.name);
});

app.get('*', function(req, res){
  res.send('Danger, Will Robinson!', 404);
});

app.listen(3000);
```

This example is similar to Example 7-6, in that we are validating whether a user exists before passing on control. However, we are not doing this only for all the subsequent routes; we are also doing it across all HTTP verbs. Normally when only one route matches, this doesn't make any difference, but it's important to note how you can pass state between routes.

When the `req.user` attribute is added in the `app.all()` method, it is available in all the subsequent methods because the middleware owns the request object. When each callback is fired, the variable `.req` is really a pointer to the request object owned by the middleware, and any changes to the request object are visible to every other function and route using the middleware.

Example 7-8 shows how a file extension can be made either optional or mandatory within a specific range. In the first `get()`, the `:format` parameter is optional (as denoted by the question mark), so Express will respond to requests for a user by ID, regardless of which format has been requested. It is up to the programmer to capture the formats (JSON, XML, text, etc.) via a switch statement in order to do special processing.

In the second example, the `:format` parameter looks for `json` or `xml` as predefined file types. If those are not found, the book request will not be processed, regardless of whether the `:id` parameter is valid. This gives us greater control over which requests are responded to and ensures that only formats for which a view can be generated are available to respond.

Example 7-8. Optional and required route extensions

```
var express = require('express');
var app = express.createServer();

app.get('/users/:id.:format?', function(req, res) {
  res.send(req.params.id + "<br/>" + req.params.format);
  // Responds to:
  // /users/15
  // /users/15.xml
  // /users/15.json
});

app.get('/books/:id.:format((json|xml))', function(req, res) {
  res.send(req.params.id + "<br/>" + req.params.format);
  // Responds to:
  // /books/7.json
  // /books/7.xml
  // But NOT to:
  // /books/7
  // /books/7.txt
});

app.listen(8080);
```

Handling Form Data

Most examples have demonstrated the GET verb, but Express is built to support RESTful architecture in the style of Ruby on Rails. Using hidden fields inside web forms, you can indicate whether a form's intention is to PUT (replace data), POST (create data), DELETE (remove data) or GET (retrieve data). See Example 7-9.

Example 7-9. Handling forms using Express

```
var express = require('express');
var app = express.createServer();

app.use(express.limit('1mb'));
app.use(express.bodyParser());
app.use(express.methodOverride());

app.get('/', function(req, res) {
  res.send('<form method="post" action="/">' +
           '<input type="hidden" name="_method" value="put" />' +
           'Your Name: <input type="text" name="username" />' +
           '<input type="submit" />' +
           '</form>');
});

app.put('/', function(req, res) {
  res.send('Welcome, ' + req.body.username);
});

app.listen(8080);
```

This simple application demonstrates the use of a form. First, an Express application is created and configured to use the bodyParser() and methodOverride() functions. The bodyParser() function parses the request body sent by the web browser and translates form variables into objects usable by Express. The methodOverride() function allows the hidden _method variable in form posts to override the GET method in favor of the RESTful method types.

The express.limit() function instructs Express to limit the length of request bodies to 1 MB. This is an important security consideration because otherwise it would be possible to send a large post to the application to be processed by bodyParser(), making it very easy to launch a denial-of-service (DoS) attack.

 Be sure to call methodOverride() after bodyParser(). Otherwise, the form variables will not be processed when Express checks to see whether it should be responding to a GET or some other command.

Template Engines

Clearly, it isn't practical to continue writing HTML directly in application code. For starters, it is unreadable and unmaintainable; but more importantly, it is bad form to mix application logic with presentation markup. Template engines allow developers space to focus on how to present information to the user—often in different formats, such as screen or mobile—and inject specific data separately from processing.

Express is minimalist and does not come with built-in template engines, opting instead for community-supported modules. Some of the more popular engines are Haml, Jade, Embedded Javascript (EJ), CoffeeKup (a CoffeeScript-based engine), and jQuery templates.

In Example 7-10, an application is set up to render a simple Jade template.

Example 7-10. Using a basic Jade template in Express

```
var express = require('express');
var app = express.createServer();

app.get('/', function(req, res) {
  res.render('index.jade', { pageTitle: 'Jade Example', layout: false });
});

app.listen(8080);
```

To run this example, you will need to install the Jade template engine:

```
npm install jade
```

The first thing to notice is the lack of any reference to the Jade library. Express parses the view template's filename and uses the extension (in this case, the `jade` from *index.jade*) to determine which view engine should be used. Therefore, it is possible to mix and match different view engines into the same project. You are not limited to using only Jade or only CoffeeKup, for example; you can use both.

This example passes two arguments into the render function. The first is the name of the view to display, and the second contains options and variables needed for the rendering. We'll come back to the filename in a minute. There are two variables passed into the view in this example: `pageTitle` and `layout`. The `layout` variable is interesting in this case because it is set to `false`, which instructs the Jade view engine to render the contents of *index.jade* without first going through a master layout file (more on this later).

`pageTitle` is a local variable that will be consumed by the contents of the view. It represents the point of templating: whereas the HTML is specified mostly in *index.jade* file, that file has a placeholder named `pageTitle` where Jade will plug in the value we provide.

The file (*index.jade*) from the first parameter needs to be placed in the *views* folder (*/views/index.jade*) and looks like Example 7-11.

Example 7-11. A basic Jade file for Express

```
!!! 5
html(lang="en")
  head
    title =pageTitle
  body
    h1 Hello, World
    p This is an example of Jade.
```

After Jade plugs in the value for `pageTitle` that we supplied, the page renders as:

```
<!DOCTYPE html>
<html lang="en">
  <head>
    <title>Jade Example</title>
  </head>

  <body>
    <h1>Hello, World</h1>
    <p>This is an example of Jade.</p>
  </body>
</html>
```

The Jade template aims to make the page more succinct by paring down the markup to the bare minimum. Instead of the closing tags you may be accustomed to in HTML, Jade uses indentation to communicate position within the page's hierarchy, resulting in a clean and generally easy-to-read file.

The very first line, "!!! 5", identifies the content type as HTML5, manifesting as an HTML5 doctype in the resulting output. The default document types supported by Jade are 5, xml, default (which is XHTML 1.0 Transitional), transitional (the default), strict, frameset, 1.1, basic, and mobile. You can supply your own, though, such as doctype html PUBLIC "-//W3C//DATA XHTML Custom 1.10a//DE".

Look in the title tag on the fourth line of the Jade input. The string =pageTitle is interpreted by Jade as "insert the contents of the variable named pageTitle here." In the resulting output, this becomes Jade Example, the value provided by the previous application code.

As we mentioned, there are many other templating options, each of which does essentially what Jade does, but with different syntax and conventions.

Layouts and partial views

Layouts allow views to share common structural elements in your site, providing an even greater separation of content and data. By standardizing parts of the layout, such as navigation, header, and footer, you can focus your development efforts on the actual content for each view.

Example 7-12 takes the view engine concept already discussed and turns it into a "real" website.

Example 7-12. Defining global template engines in Express

```
var express = require('express');
var app = express.createServer();

app.set('view engine', 'jade');

app.get('/', function(req, res) {
  res.render('battlestar')
});
```

New to this example is the set command on the "view engine" parameter. The Jade view engine will now be considered the default by Express, although it is still possible to override it in the render method.

The render function is markedly different. Because the Jade engine has been set as the default view engine, this example does not need to specify the full filename, so battlestar actually refers to */views/battlestar.jade*. The layout: false parameter from Example 7-10 is no longer needed, because this time Express will be making use of this layout file located at *views/layout.jade*, shown in Example 7-13.

Example 7-13. A Jade layout file in Express

```
html
  body
    h1 Battlestar Galactica Fan Page
    != body
```

The layout file is very similar to the view file created earlier, but in this case there is a special **body** variable. We're talking here about the != **body** line; please don't confuse that with the **body** keyword near the top of the file. The second **body** is not the name of a variable passed in through the application code, so where does it come from?

When the **layout** option is set to **true** (the default) in Express, the **render** method works by parsing the contents of the first parameter and passing the rendered output to the layout as a variable called **body**. The *battlestar.jade* file looks like Example 7-14.

Example 7-14. A Jade partial view in Express

```
p Welcome to the fan page.
```

This is called a partial view because it does not contain the full content needed to generate a page, and it needs to be combined with a layout to become useful output. The final web browser output for all this work looks like this:

```
<html>
  <body>
    <h1>Battlestar Galactica Fan Page</h1>
    <p>Welcome to the fan page.</p>
  </body>
</html>
```

Partial views are powerful because they allow developers to focus on the specific content being displayed, rather than the web page as a whole. This means the contents don't have to be tied to a web page and can be output to mobile web pages, AJAX requests (for in-place page refreshes), and more.

 Be careful not to confuse the variable named **body**, which contains the actual content of your view, with the keyword **body**, which is an HTML tag used by the web browser.

Middleware

Some of the examples up to this point have included a rather innocuous-looking function: **app.use()**. This function invokes the Connect library and exposes many powerful tools that make it simple to add functionality. Now it's time to take a step back and examine what all this glue—known as middleware—is, and why it is so important to developing with Express.

Although it might sound like one of those obscure buzzwords that programmers like to use when they want to appear "in the know," middleware—as we've mentioned in previous chapters—refers to a piece of software that acts as a link between two other programs, typically between a higher-level application and a wider network. In the real world, middleware is analogous to the telephone lines you might find in your home or office building. All telephones (applications) connect to the same telephone lines (middleware), which in turn broker communication from the application to the underlying network.

Your phone may or may not support call waiting or voicemail, but the line behaves the same, regardless of which features are available to you. You may have voicemail built into your phone, or it may be provided by your telco (network); in either case, the line itself is happy to support your usage.

Connect provides the middleware functionality used by Express (see Table 7-1). As shown in Figure 7-1, Connect extends Node's base http module, giving it all of the base capabilities provided by http, upon which it adds its own functionality. Express in turn inherits from Connect, gaining its abilities and, by extension, http's as well. Any module plugged into Connect is automatically made available to Express. Connect is the middle layer between Express and the network, and as such exposes and uses a myriad of features that may not be used directly by Express, but are available all the same. Finally, because Express derives itself from Connect, most of Connect's functionality is available directly from Express, allowing you to issue commands such as app.body Parser() rather than connect.bodyParser().

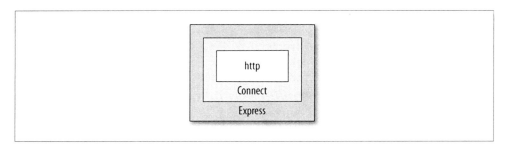

Figure 7-1. Express's middleware stack

Table 7-1. Middleware bundled with Connect

Name	Description
basicAuth	Accepts a callback function that accepts username and password parameters, then returns true if the credentials are permitted access to the site.
bodyParser	Parses the contents of the request body.
compiler	Compiles *.sass* and *.less* files to CSS and CoffeeScript files to JavaScript.
.cookieParser	Parses the contents of cookies sent by the web browser in the request headers.
csrf	Provides cross-site request forgery (CSRF) protection by mutating the request through an additional form variable. Requires session and bodyParser middleware.
directory	Prints directory listings inside a root path, with options to display hidden files and icons.
errorHandler	Traps errors encountered by the application and provides options to log errors to stderr or request output in multiple formats (JSON, plain text, or HTML).
favicon	Serves favicon files from memory, with cache control.

Name	Description
limit	Limits the size of requests accepted by the server to protect against DoS attacks.
logger	Logs requests to output or a file, in multiple formats, either on response (default) or on request. Optional buffer size controls how many requests are collected before writing to disk.
methodOverride	Combine with bodyParser to provide DELETE and PUT methods along with POST. Allows for more explicit route definitions; for example, use app.put() rather than detecting the user's intention from app.post(). This technique enables RESTful application design.
profiler	Typically placed before all other middleware, profiler records the response time and memory statistics for requests.
query	Parses query strings and populates the req.query parameter.
responseTime	Populates the X-Response-Time header with the time (in milliseconds) to generate a response.
router	Provides advanced routing (discussed in "Setting Up Routes in Express" on page 146)
session	The session manager for persisting user data across requests.
static	Enables streaming of static files from a root directory. Allows for partial downloads and custom expiry aging.
staticCache	Adds a caching layer to the static middleware, keeping the most popular downloaded files in memory for greatly improved response times.
vhost	Enables multiple sites for different vhosts on a single machine.

Middleware factories

By now you may have noticed that middleware consists of little more than functions that are executed sequentially by Express. JavaScript closures give us a lot of power to implement the factory pattern[3] inside Node, which can be exploited to provide contextual functionality to your web routes.

Express's routing functions use internal middleware during their processing cycle, which you can override to add extra functionality—for example, to add custom headers to your HTML output. Let's look at Example 7-15 and see how we can use a middleware factory to intercept a page request and enforce role-based authentication.

Example 7-15. Middleware factories in Express

```
var express = require('express');
var app = express.createServer(
  express.cookieParser(),
  express.session({ secret: 'secret key' })
);

var roleFactory = function(role) {
  return function(req, res, next) {
    if ( req.session.role && req.session.role.indexOf(role) != -1 ) {
      next();
```

---

3. A *factory* is an object that creates other objects with specific parameters, whereas creating those objects manually would involve a lot of repetitive or complex program code.

```
    } else {
      res.send('You are not authenticated.');
    }
  }
};

app.get('/', roleFactory('admin'), function(req, res) {
  res.send('Welcome to Express!');
});

app.get('/auth', function(req, res) {
  req.session.role = 'admin';
  res.send('You have been authenticated.');
});

app.listen(8080);
```

Right off the bat, if you visit *http://localhost:8080/* you will receive the message "You are not authenticated." However, if you look at the contents of the route for `'/'`, you will notice that the actual page contents are `'Welcome to Express!'`. The second parameter, `roleFactory('admin')`, launched before the page was displayed and detected that there was no `role` property in your session, so it output its own message and stopped the page execution.

If you visit *http://localhost:8080/auth* followed by *http://localhost:8080/* you will receive the "Welcome to Express!" message. In this circumstance, the */auth* URL attached the `'admin'` variable to your session's role property, so when `roleFactory` was executed it passed the execution control to `next()`, which is the `app.get('/')` function.

Therefore, it could be said that by using internal middleware, we changed the order of execution to:

1. roleFactory('admin')
2. app.get('/')

What if we wanted to authenticate based on more than one role? In that case, we could change the route to:

```
var powerUsers = [roleFactory('admin'),roleFactory('client')];
app.get('/', powerUsers, function(req, res) {
  res.send('Welcome to Express!');
});
```

Because we passed an array as the middleware, we have limited the page execution to users belonging to the "admin" and "client" roles, and changed the order of execution to:

1. roleFactory('admin')
2. roleFactory('client')
3. app.get('/')

Because each `roleFactory` demands that the role be present in the session, the user must be both a "client" and an "admin" in order to access the page.

Socket.IO

Socket.IO is a simple little library that's a lot like Node's core net library. Socket.IO allows you to send messages back and forth with browser clients that connect with your Node server, using an efficient, low-level socket mechanism. One of the nice things about the module is that it provides a shared interface between the browser and the server. That is, you can write the same JavaScript on both in order to do messaging work once you have a connection established.

Socket.IO is so named because it supports the HTML5 WebSockets standard on browsers that support it (and have it enabled). Fortunately, the library also supports a number of fallbacks:

- WebSocket
- WebSocket over Flash
- XHR Polling
- XHR Multipart Streaming
- Forever Iframe
- JSONP Polling

These options ensure that you'll be able to have some kind of persistent connection to the browser in almost any environment. The Socket.IO module includes the code to power these connection paths on both the browser and the server side with the same API.

Instantiating Socket.IO is as simple as including the module and creating a server. One of the things that's a little different about Socket.IO is that it requires an HTTP server as well; see Example 7-16.

Example 7-16. Creating a Socket.IO server

```
    var http = require('http'),
    io = require('socket.io');

server = http.createServer();
server.on('request', function(req, res){
  //Typical HTTP server stuff
  res.writeHead(200, {'Content-Type': 'text/plain'});
  res.end('Hello World');
});

server.listen(80);

var socket = io.listen(server);
```

```
socket.on('connection', function(client){
  console.log('Client connected');
});
```

The HTTP server in this example could do anything. In this case, we simply return "Hello World." However, Socket.IO doesn't care what the HTTP server will do; it simply wraps its own event listener around all requests to your server. This listener will look for any requests for Socket.IO's client libraries and service these requests. It passes on all others to be handled by the HTTP server, which will function as usual.

The example creates a `socket.io` server by calling `io.listen()`, which is a factory method for the `Listener` class. `listen()` takes a function as an argument, which it uses as a callback when a client connects to the server. Because the sockets are persistent connections, you aren't dealing with a `req` and `res` object as you do with an HTTP server. As with `net`, you need to use the passed `client` object to communicate with each browser. Of course, it's also important to have some code in the browser (Example 7-17) to interact with the server.

Example 7-17. A small web page to interact with a Socket.IO server

```
<!DOCTYPE html>
<html>
  <body>
    <script src="/socket.io/socket.io.js"></script>
    <script>
      var socket = io.connect('http://localhost:8080');
      socket.on('message', function(data){ console.log(data) })
    </script>
  </body>
</html>
```

This simple page starts by loading the necessary Socket.IO client library directly from the Node server, which is localhost on port 8080 in this case.

 Although port 80 is the standard HTTP port, port 8080 is more convenient during development because many developers run web servers locally for testing that would interfere with Node's work. In addition, many Linux systems have built-in security policies preventing nonadministrator users from using port 80, so it is more convenient to use a higher number.

Next, we create a new `Socket` object with the hostname of the Socket.IO server we are connecting to. We ask the `Socket` to connect with `socket.connect()`. Then we add a listener for the `message` event. Notice how the API is like a Node API. Whenever the server sends this client a message, the client will output it to the browser's console window.

Now let's modify our server to send this page to clients so we can test it (Example 7-18).

Example 7-18. A simple Socket.IO server

```
    var http = require('http'),
    io = require('socket.io'),
    fs = require('fs');

var sockFile = fs.readFileSync('socket.html');

server = http.createServer();
server.on('request', function(req, res){
  res.writeHead(200, {'content-type': 'text/html'});
  res.end(sockFile);
});

server.listen(8080);

var socket = io.listen(server);

socket.on('connection', function(client){
  console.log('Client connected');
  client.send('Welcome client ' + client.sessionId);
});
```

The most striking change in this example is the addition of the `fs.readFileSync` function, which brings the web page's external file into the socket server. Now instead of responding to web browser requests with "Hello World," the Node server will respond with the contents of *socket.html*. Because `readFileSync` is a synchronous function, it will block Node's event loop until the file is read, ensuring that the file is ready to be delivered to clients immediately when the server becomes available for connections.

Now whenever anyone requests anything from the server, unless it is a request to the Socket.IO client library, he will get a copy of *socket.html* (which might be the code in Example 7-17). The callback for connections has been extended to send a welcome message to clients, and a client running the code from Example 7-18 might get a message in its console like `Welcome client 17844937089830637`. Each client gets its own `sessionId`. Currently, the ID is an integer generated using `Math.random()`.

Namespaces

Creating websockets as shown is fine when you are in full control of your application and architecture, but this will quickly lead to conflicts when you are attaching them to an existing application that uses sockets or when you are writing a service to be plugged into someone else's project. Example 7-19 demonstrates how namespaces avoid this problem by effectively dividing Socket.IO's listeners into channels.

Example 7-19. A modified web page to interact with Socket.IO namespaces

```
<!DOCTYPE html>
<html>
  <body>
    <script src="/socket.io/socket.io.js"></script>
```

```
    <script>
      var upandrunning = io.connect('http://localhost:8080/upandrunning');
      var weather = io.connect('http://localhost:8080/weather');
      upandrunning.on('message', function(data){
        document.write('<br /><br />Node: Up and Running Update<br />');
        document.write(data);
      });
      weather.on('message', function(data){
        document.write('<br /><br />Weather Update<br />');
        document.write(data);
      });
    </script>
  </body>
</html>
```

This updated *socket.html* makes two Socket.IO connections, one to *http://localhost:8080/upandrunning* and the other to *http://localhost:8080/weather*. Each connection has its own variable and its own `.on()` event listener. Apart from these differences, working with Socket.IO remains the same. Instead of logging to the console, Example 7-20 displays its message results within the web browser window.

Example 7-20. A namespace-enabled Socket.IO server

```
var sockFile = fs.readFileSync('socket.html');

server = http.createServer();
server.on('request', function(req, res){
  res.writeHead(200, {'content-type': 'text/html'});
  res.end(sockFile);
});

server.listen(8080);

var socket = io.listen(server);

socket.of('/upandrunning')
  .on('connection', function(client){
    console.log('Client connected to Up and Running namespace.');
    client.send("Welcome to 'Up and Running'");
});

socket.of('/weather')
  .on('connection', function(client){
    console.log('Client connected to Weather namespace.');
    client.send("Welcome to 'Weather Updates'");
});
```

The function `socket.of` splits the socket object into multiple unique namespaces, each with its own rules for handling connections. If a client were to connect to *http://localhost:8080/weather* and issue an `emit()` command, its results would be processed only within that namespace, and not within the */upandrunning* namespace.

Using Socket.IO with Express

There are many cases where you would want to use Socket.IO by itself within Node as its own application or as a component of a larger website architecture that includes non-Node components. However, when it's used as part of a full Node application using Express, you can gain an enormous amount of efficiency by writing the entire software stack—including the client-facing views—in the same language (JavaScript).

Save Example 7-21 as *socket_express.html*.

Example 7-21. Attaching Socket.IO to an Express application: client code

```
<script src="/socket.io/socket.io.js"></script>
<script>
var socket = io.connect('http://localhost:8080');
socket.on('news', function(data) {
  document.write('<h1>' + data.title + '</h1>' );
  document.write('<p>' + data.contents + '</p>' );
  if ( data.allowResponse ) {
    socket.emit('scoop', { contents: 'News data received by client.' });
  }
});
</script>
```

This example starts by connecting to the Socket.IO on port 8080. Whenever the Socket.IO server sends a "news" event, the client writes the new item's title and contents to the browser page. If the news item allows a response, the client socket emits a "scoop" event. The scoop wouldn't be very interesting to a real reporter; it only contains an acknowledgment that the client received the original news.

This being an example press, the news server responds to the "scoop" event by emitting another news story. The client will receive this new story and print it to the screen also. To prevent this cycle from continuing out of control, an `allowResponse` parameter is sent with the news story. If it is false or not present at all (see Example 7-22), the client will not send a scoop.

Example 7-22 shows the Express server.

Example 7-22. Attaching Socket.IO to an Express application: server code

```
var app = require('express').createServer(),
    io = require('socket.io').listen(app);

app.listen(8080);

app.get('/', function(req,res) {
  res.sendfile(__dirname + '/socket_express.html');
});

io.sockets.on('connection', function(socket) {
  socket.emit('news', {
    title: 'Welcome to World News',
```

```
    contents: 'This news flash was sent from Node.js!',
    allowResponse: true
  });
  socket.on('scoop', function(data) {
    socket.emit('news', {
      title: 'Circular Emissions Worked',
      contents: 'Received this content: ' + data.contents
    });
  });
});
```

The Express server is created first and then passed into Socket.IO as a parameter. When the Express application is started with the `listen()` function, both the web server and socket server are activated. Next, a route for the base path (/) is defined as a pass-through for sending the client-side file created in Example 7-21.

The server-side code for the news broadcaster looks very similar to the client-side code for good reason. The same events (emit, on message, connection) behave similarly in Node and in the web browser, making connectivity straightforward. Because data is passed as JavaScript objects between both endpoints, no additional parsing or serialization is needed.

Clearly, we can very quickly gain a lot of power by plugging Socket.IO into Express, but astute programmers will realize that this is one-way communication of limited value, unless the connection initiated by the user's web browser is represented in the socket stream. Any changes (logout, profile settings, etc.) should be reflected in any socket actions, and vice versa. How to accomplish that? Sessions.

To illustrate the use of a session for authentication, let's look first at the client-side code, *views/socket.html*, shown in Example 7-23.

Example 7-23. Client HTML (Jade template): Socket.IO sessions

```
!!! 5
html(lang='en')
  head
    script(type='text/javascript', src='/socket.io/socket.io.js')
    script(type='text/javascript')
      var socket = io.connect('http://localhost:8080');
      socket.on('emailchanged', function(data) {
        document.getElementById('email').value = data.email;
      });
      var submitEmail = function(form) {
        socket.emit('emailupdate', {email: form.email.value});
        return false;
      };
  body
    h1 Welcome!

    form(onsubmit='return submitEmail(this);')
      input(id='email', name='email', type='text', value=locals.email)
      input(type='submit', value='Change Email')
```

When rendered in a web browser, this page will display a form text box with a "Change Email" call to action whose default value comes from Express's session data through the `locals.email` variable. Upon user input, the application performs these actions:

1. Create a Socket.IO connection and send all of the user's email updates as an `emailupdate` event.

2. Listen for `emailchanged` events and replace the contents of the text box with the new email from the server (more on this soon).

Next, have a look at the Node.js portion of Example 7-24.

Example 7-24. Sharing session data between Express and Socket.IO

```
var io = require('socket.io');
var express = require('express');
var app = express.createServer();
var store = new express.session.MemoryStore;
var utils = require('connect').utils;
var Session = require('connect').middleware.session.Session;

app.configure(function() {
  app.use(express.cookieParser());
  app.use(express.session({secret: 'secretKey', key: 'express.sid', store: store}));
  app.use(function(req, res) {
    var sess = req.session;
    res.render('socket.jade', {
      email: sess.email || ''
    });
  });
});

// Start the app
app.listen(8080);

var sio = io.listen(app);

sio.configure(function() {
  sio.set('authorization', function (data, accept ) {
    var cookies = utils.parseCookie(data.headers.cookie);
    data.sessionID = cookies['express.sid'];
    data.sessionStore = store;
    store.get(data.sessionID, function(err, session) {
      if ( err || !session ) {
        return accept("Invalid session", false);
      }
      data.session = new Session(data, session);
      accept(null,true);
    });
  });

  sio.sockets.on('connection', function(socket) {
    var session = socket.handshake.session;
    socket.join(socket.handshake.sessionId);
    socket.on('emailupdate', function(data) {
```

```
      session.email = data.email;
      session.save();
      sio.sockets.in(socket.handshake.sessionId).emit('emailchanged', {
        email: data.email
      });
    });
  });
});
```

This example uses Connect, a middleware framework that simplifies common tasks such as session management, working with cookies, authentication, caching, performance metrics, and more. In this example, the cookie and session tools are used to manipulate user data. Socket.IO is not aware of Express and vice versa, so Socket.IO is not aware of sessions when the user connects. However, both components need to use the Session object to share data. This is an excellent demonstration of the Separation of Concerns (SoC) programming paradigm.[4]

This example demonstrates using Socket.IO's authorization, even after connection, to parse the user's headers. Because the session ID is passed to the server as a cookie, you can use this value to read Express's session ID.

This time, the Express setup includes a line for session management. The arguments used to build the session manager are a secret key (used to prevent session tampering), the session key (used to store the session ID in the web browser's cookie), and a store object (used to store session data for later retrieval). The store object is the most important. Instead of letting Express create and manage the memory store, this example creates a variable and passes it into Express. Now the session store is available to the entire application, not just Express.

Next, a route is created for the default (/) web page. In previous Socket.IO examples, this function was used to output HTML directly to the web browser. This time, Express will render the contents of *views/socket.jade* to the web browser. The second variable in render() is the email address stored in the session, which is interpreted and used as the default text field value in Example 7-23.

The real action happens in Socket.IO's 'authorization' event. When the web browser connects to the server, Socket.IO performs an authentication routine to determine whether the connection should proceed. The criteria in this case is a valid session, which was provided by Express when the user loaded the web page. Socket.IO reads the session ID from the request headers using parseCookie (part of the Connect framework), loads the session from the memory store, and creates a Session object with the information it receives.

---

4. SoC refers to the practice of breaking down software into smaller single-purpose parts (concerns) that have as little overlapping functionality as possible. Middleware enables this style of design by allowing totally separate modules to interact in a common environment without needing to be aware of each other. Although, as we have seen with modules such as bodyParser(), it remains up to the programmer to understand how the concerns ultimately interact and use them in the appropriate order and context.

The data passed to the authorization event is stored in the socket's handshake property. Therefore, saving the session object into the data object makes it available later in the socket's lifecycle. When creating the Session object, use the memory store that was created and passed into Express; now both Express and Socket.IO are able to access the same session data—Express by manipulating the req.session object, and sockets by manipulating the socket.handshake.session object.

Assuming all goes well, calling accept() authenticates the socket and allows the connection to continue.

Now suppose the user accesses your site from more than one tab in his web browser. There would be two connections from the same session created, so how would you handle events that need to update connected sockets? Socket.IO provides support for *rooms*, or *channels* if you prefer. By initiating a join() command with sessionId as the argument in Example 7-24, the socket transparently created a dedicated channel you can use to send messages to all connections currently in use by that user. Logging out is an obvious use for this technique: when the user logs out from one tab, the logout command will instantly transmit to all the others, leaving all of the user's views of the application in a consistent state.

 Always remember to execute session.save() after changing session data. Otherwise, the changes will not be reflected on subsequent requests.

## CHAPTER 8

Extending Node

Modules

The module system in Node makes it easy to create extensions to the platform. It is simple to learn and enables us to easily share reusable library code. The Node module system is based on the commonJS module specification. We've already used lots of modules in the previous chapters, but here we'll study how to create our own modules. Example 8-1 shows one simple implementation.

Example 8-1. A simple module

```
exports.myMethod = function() { console.log('Method output') };
exports.property = "blue";
```

As you can see, writing a module is as simple as attaching properties to the `exports` global variable. Any script that is included with `require()` will return its `exports` object. This means that everything returned from `require()` is in a closure, so you can use private variables in a module that are not exposed to the main scope of the program.

Node developers have created a few conventions around modules. First, it's typical to create factory methods for a class. Although you might also expose the class itself, factory methods give us a clean way to instantiate objects. For I/O-related classes, one of the arguments is normally a callback for either the I/O being done or one of its most common aspects. For example, `http.Server` has a factory method called `http.create Server()` that takes a callback function for the `request` event, the most commonly used `http.Server` event.

Package Manager

Being able to make modules is great, but ultimately having a good way to distribute them and share them with the rest of your team or the community is essential. The package manager for Node, npm, provides a way of distributing code, either locally or via a global repository of Node modules. npm helps you manage code dependencies, installation, and other things associated with distributing code. Best of all, npm is all JavaScript and Node. So if you are already using Node, you are ready to use npm, too. npm provides both the installation tools for developers and the distribution tools for package maintainers.

Most developers will start by using npm to install packages using the simple npm install command. You can install packages you have locally, but you'll probably want to use npm to install remote packages from the npm registry. The registry stores packages that other Node developers make available to you to use. There are many packages in the registry: everything from database drivers to flow control libraries to math libraries. Most things you'll install with npm are 100% JavaScript, but a few of them require compilation. Luckily, npm will do that for you. You can see what's in the registry at *http://search.npmjs.org*.

Searching Packages

The search command lists all packages in the global npm registry and filters for a package name:

```
npm search packagename
```

If you don't supply a package name, all of the available packages will be displayed.

If the package list is out of date (because you added or removed a package, or you know the package you want should be available but it isn't), you can instruct npm to clean the cache using the following command:

```
npm cache clean
```

The next time you ask npm for a list of packages, the command will take longer because it will need to rebuild its cache.

Creating Packages

Although most of the packages you get using the npm install command are available to anyone who uses Node, writing a package does not require publishing it to the world. Consolidating your own code into module packages makes it easy to reuse your work across multiple projects, share it with other developers, or make it available to staging or production servers running your application.

Packages do not have to be limited to modules or extensions; in many cases, packages contain full applications intended for deployment. Package files make deployment easy by declaring dependencies, eliminating the library-labyrinth guesswork that was traditionally required when moving from development to production environments.

Creating a package doesn't require much more work than creating a *package.json* file with some basic definitions about your module—its name and version number being the most critical components. To quickly generate a valid package file, run the command `npm init` from your module's directory. You will be prompted to enter descriptive information about your module. Then the command will emit a *packages.json* file into the directory. If a package file already exists, its attributes will be used as the default values and you will be given a chance to overwrite them with new information.

To use your package, install it using `npm install /path/to/yourpackage`. The path may be a directory on your filesystem or an external URL (such as GitHub).

Publishing Packages

If your module is useful to a broader audience and ready for prime time, you can release it to the world using npm's `publish` command. To publish the contents of your package:

1. Create a user with the `adduser` command:

    ```
    npm adduser
    ```

    Follow the instructions that appear. You will be prompted for a username, password, and email address.

2. Publish your package with the `publish` command:

    ```
    npm publish
    ```

That's all there is to the process. At present, no registration or validation is needed.

 This raises an interesting point about npm: because anyone can publish a package without any prefiltering or oversight, the quality of the libraries you install using npm is uncertain. So "buyer beware."

If you decide later to unpublish your package, you may do so with the `npm unpublish` command. Note that you will need to clear your package list cache.

Linking

Although npm excels at publishing and deploying, it was designed primarily as a tool for managing dependencies during development. The `npm link` command creates a symbolic link between your project and its dependencies, so any changes in the dependencies are available to you as you work on your project.

There are two major reasons you would want to do this:

- You want to use `requires()` to access one of your projects from another one of your projects.
- You want to use the same package in multiple projects, without needing to maintain its version in each of your projects.

Typing npm link with no arguments creates a symbolic link for the current project inside the global packages path, making it available to npm in all other projects on your system. To use this feature, you need to have a *packages.json* file, described earlier. Using npm init is the fastest way to generate a barebones version of this file.

Typing npm link *packagename* creates a symbolic link from the project's working directory to the global modules path for that package. For example, typing npm link express will install the Express framework in the global packages directory and include it in your project. Whenever Express is updated, your project will automatically use the latest version from the global packages directory. If you have linked Express in more than one project, all of those projects will be synchronized to the most recent version, freeing you from having to update every one of them whenever Express is updated.

Add-ons

Whereas modules are the JavaScript extensions for Node, *add-ons* are the C/C++ extensions. Add-ons frequently wrap existing system libraries and expose their functionality to Node. They can, of course, create new functionality too, although most people choose to do that in JavaScript for obvious reasons. Add-ons are dynamically linked shared objects.

To create an add-on, you'll need at least two sets of files: the add-on code and the build files. Node uses the waf build system written in Python. Let's start with a "Hello World" example. Example 8-2 is equivalent to exports.hello = "world"; in JavaScript.

Example 8-2. A simple add-on for Node

```
#include <v8.h>

using namespace v8;

extern "C" void init (Handle<Object> target) {
  HandleScope scope;
  target->Set(String::New("hello"), String::New("world"));
}
```

The first thing this code needs to do is include the **v8** header file because Node is built on top of V8. This provides a lot of standard objects that we will use. Next, we declare the namespace. Then we create the *wrapper*, which is required by all add-ons. The wrapper functions like the exports global variable for JavaScript modules. We'll hang everything we expose from the add-on off a function with the signature extern 'C' void init (Handle<Object> target).

Glossary

Blocking operation

A blocking operation requires the program to halt while it is waiting for a slow resource.

Typically, this is either a hardware resource (such as a disk drive), or a network resource (such as an HTTP request). Because the request cannot require a result from a slow resource, it blocks subsequent operation until it is complete, even if the computer or program still has available resources such as CPU or memory available.

Callback

A callback is a function that is "called back" to after a blocking operation. Typically, this is an I/O operation such as disk access. Callbacks can take parameters.

Class

See Pseudoclass.

Function

A unit of code that can be invoked with a set of variable parameters. It may pass a single return. In JavaScript, functions also have a *context*, which defines the value of the reserved this variable. Functions in JavaScript are considered *first class* in that they can also be treated as variables or properties of objects.

Method

A function that is a property of an object.

See also Function.

Nonblocking operation

A nonblocking operation is one that does not block.

See also Blocking operation.

Pseudoclass

A pseudoclass is a way of creating an abtract object in JavaScript that is intended to be initialized into an object. Pseudoclasses should be turned into objects using the new keyword. Pseudoclass names start with a leading capital by convention to differentiate them from other kinds of objects. For example, Server would be a pseudoclass, and server might be an instance of that pseudoclass.

Index

Symbols

. (period), 8

A

A (address) records, 77
accept HTTP header, 31
add-ons, 172
address (A) records, 77
advanced message queueing protocol (AMQP),
    140–143
aes192 algorithm, 83
Almaer, Dion, 13
AMQP (advanced message queueing protocol),
    140–143
APIs, 55
    (see also specific APIs)
    adding, 25
    core, 55–76
    helper, 77–106
    testing, 26
applications (see web applications)
apt command, 127
ASCII encoding format, 73, 74
assert module
    about, 27, 101–104
    deepEqual() method, 102
    doesNotThrow() method, 102
    equal() method, 101
    notDeepEqual() method, 102
    notEqual() method, 101
    notStringEqual() method, 102
    strictEqual() method, 28
    stringEqual() method, 102
    throws() method, 102

asynchronous communications
    callbacks and modified objects, 44
    error handling in, 46
    fs module and, 69
    I/O activities and, 41
auth command (Redis), 122
authentication, password (Redis), 122

B

basicAuth middleware, 156
binary data
    about, 71–73
    strings and, 73
block ciphers, 83
blocking operations, 173
blowfish algorithm, 83
bodyParser middleware, 26, 152, 156
browsers (see web browsers)
BSON object storage, 123
Buffer class
    about, 3, 17, 63, 70
    binary data and, 71–73
    binary data and strings, 73
    byteLength() method, 75
    size considerations, 71, 74
    toString() method, 17
    usage considerations, 73–75
    working with strings, 75–76
    write() method, 75

C

callbacks
    dealing with events, 57–59
    defined, 10, 173

We'd like to hear your suggestions for improving our indexes. Send email to *index@oreilly.com*.

175

Hmac class, 81, 82
Sign class, 82, 85
Verify class, 82, 86
cryptography
    hashing and, 79–81
    HMAC and, 79, 81–82
    OpenSSL and, 5, 81
    public key, 82–86
    usage considerations, 79
CSRF (cross-site request forgery) protection,
        156
csrf middleware, 156

D

Dahl, Ryan, 59
data access
    about, 107
    connection pooling, 137–139
    CouchDB database, 107–115
    MongoDB database, 123–127
    MQ protocols, 139–143
    MySQL database system, 127–133
    PostgreSQL database system, 134–136
    Redis key-value store, 115–122
data event, 69
db-mysql package, 127
Decipher class
    about, 82, 84
    update() method, 84
.delete command (MySQL), 131
DELETE verb (HTTP), 109, 151
deleting
    data in MySQL, 130
    data in PostgreSQL, 136
    documents from CouchDB, 114
    files, 70
denial-of-service (DoS) attack, 152
die event, 38
directory middleware, 156
distributing work example, 48–52
dns module
    about, 77
    lookup() method, 78
    resolve() method, 77–79
    resolve4() method, 78
    resolve6() method, 78
    resolveMX() method, 78
    reverse() method, 77
DNS requests, 72

document stores
    CouchDB over HTTP, 108–111
    reading documents, 113
    Redis key-value store, 115–122
DOS (denial-of-service) attack, 152

E

EADDRINUSE exception, 48
Eich, Brendan, 12
EJ (Embedded JavaScript) template engine,
        152
EJS layout file, 29
emailchanged event, 165
emailupdate event, 165
Embedded JavaScript (EJ) template engine,
        152
encoding formats, 72, 74
end event, 91
error event, 23, 47
error handling, 46
errorHandler middleware, 156
eval() method call, 104
event listeners
    about, 88
    calling, 57
    creating for events, 56
    firing, 57
event loop
    about, 33–40
    callbacks and, 34–40
    patterns and, 34
    process module and, 93–94
    single-threaded concept, 35
event-driven programming
    about, 34
    callbacks and, 34–40
    nonblocking operations and, 38
    patterns and, 40–44
    single-threaded concept, 35
EventEmitter class
    about, 56
    emit() method, 56, 57
    on() method, 56
    process module and, 87
    stream support, 68
events, 56
    (see also specific events)
    callback syntax, 57–59
    creating event listeners for, 56

ServerResponse class, 10
work distribution example, 48
HTTP servers
about, 59–61
creating, 39
Socket.IO library and, 160
HTTP, CouchDB over, 108–111

I

I/O activities, 41
(see also nonblocking operations)
API support, 68–76
Node approach, 34, 40
ordered serial I/O, 42–44
splitting out, 46
unbounded latency, 41
unordered parallel I/O, 41
Ingres database system, 134
(see also PostgreSQL database system)
.insert command (MySQL), 129
installing
CouchDB database, 107
CouchDB Node module, 108
db-mysql package, 127
Express module, 23, 24, 145
Mongoose library, 125
native MongoDB driver, 123
node-db module, 127
Node.js, 4–7
PostgreSQL database system, 134
RabbitMQ message broker, 140
Redis key-value store, 115
Redis Node module, 115
IPv4 address records, 78
IPv6 address records, 78

J

Jade template engine, 152–154
JavaScript
about, 3–4, 12
browser support, 12
functional scope, 43
hexadecimal notation and, 72
maximum heap size, 46
trycatch functionality, 46
weird and amusing things about, 8
jQuery template engine, 152

K

keys
PEM-encoded, 81, 83
private, 82
public, 82–86
setting, 117
kill command, 97
Koch, Peter Paul, 13
Kvaleim, Christian, 123

L

layouts and partial views, 154–155
.less files, 156
libpq-dev package, 134
limit middleware, 157
list commands in Redis, 118
Listener class, 160
logger middleware, 157
lpush command (Redis), 118

M

mail exchanger (MX) records, 77
make command, 6
master processes, 47–52
MD5 hashing algorithm, 79, 80
methodOverride middleware, 152, 157
methods (term), 173
middleware
about, 26, 155–157
Connect library and, 44, 155
factory pattern, 157–159
route, 149
MongoDB database
about, 123
defining schemas, 125
Mongoose library, 125–127
native MongoDB driver, 123
writing records, 124
Mongoose library
about, 125
defining schemas, 125
installing, 125
manipulating collections, 126
performance considerations, 127
MQ protocols
about, 139
RabbitMQ, 140–143
multicore processors, 47–52

MVCC (multi-version concurrency control), 107
MX (mail exchanger) records, 77
MySQL database system
    about, 127
    node-db module, 127–131
    Sequelize ORM, 131–134

N

namespaces, Socket.IO library, 161–162
nesting callbacks, 42, 70
net module
    about, 16
    createServer() method, 16
    Server class, 16
    Socket class, 16, 20, 23
new keyword, 56
Node module
    CouchDB database, 108, 111
    Redis key-value store, 115
Node Package Manager (see npm)
Node REPL, 7–8
node-couchdb package
    about, 111
    creating documents, 112
    deleting documents, 114
    reading documents, 113
    updating documents, 113
    working with databases, 112
node-db module
    about, 127
    connection pooling and, 137
    deleting data, 130
    inserting data, 129
    installing, 127
    selecting data, 128
    updating data, 129
Node.js
    about, 3–4
    building chat server, 15–23
    building robust applications, 33–52
    building Twitter-like application, 23–32
    core APIs, 55–76
    extending, 169–172
    installing, 4–7
    as runtime environment, 7–8
    strengths of, 11–14
    version numbers, 5
    as web servers, 9–10, 11

nonblocking operations
    API support, 68–76
    defined, 173
    error handling and, 46
    event-driven programming and, 38
    Node approach, 34
NoSQL systems
    CouchDB database, 107–115
    MongoDB database, 123–127
    Redis key-value store, 115–122
npm (Node Package Manager)
    about, 169
    adduser command, 171
    creating packages, 170
    init command, 171
    install command, 170
    installing db-mysql package, 127
    installing Express module, 24
    installing Mongoose library, 125
    link command, 171
    linking dependencies, 171
    publish command, 171
    publishing packages, 171
    search command, 170
    searching packages, 170
    unpublish command, 171

O

object relational mapper (ORM), 131–134
objects
    passing by reference, 44
    setting and enumerating, 8
    setting multiple hash values, 117
onclick event, 4
OpenSSL
    cryptography and, 5, 79
    PEM-encoded keys, 81, 83
ordered serial I/O, 42–44
ORM (object relational mapper), 131–134
os module, 48

P

parallel I/O
    combining work groups, 41
    unordered, 41
passing objects by reference, 44
password authentication (Redis), 122
patterns

About the Authors

Tom Hughes-Croucher is a developer and technology evangelist. He's worked for and with numerous well-known brands, including Yahoo!, NASA, Tesco, Walmart, MySpace, Three Telecom, and UK Channel 4. Tom has contributed to a number of web standards for the World Wide Web Consortium (W3C) and the British Standards Institute (BSI).

Mike Wilson has had the privilege of working with some of the largest and most influential brands in the world, including Disney, Microsoft, and McDonald's. He has years of web development experience, designing and building everything from small-business sites to large MMO server clusters hosting millions of players. In his free time, Mike maintains his personal blog (*http://www.alwaysgetbetter.com*), contributes to forums, and experiments with emerging frameworks and software. Mike lives in Vancouver with his wife and their three children.

Colophon

The animal on the cover of *Node: Up and Running* is a common tree shrew (*Tupaia glis*). These arboreal mammals are found in the southern parts of Southeast Asia. Common tree shrews live in forests, though they are also found in orchards and gardens. They are good climbers and can jump up to two feet between trees. They are active during the day, feeding on plants, seeds, and fruit, as well as ants, spiders, and small lizards.

Common tree shrews are 6–8 inches long, with a thick bushy tail as long as their bodies. They have pointed snouts and five-toed clawed feet. Their fur is black, gray, or reddish, with white on the belly. The genus name *Tupaia* comes from the Malay for "squirrel," which the creatures somewhat resemble. Tree shrews were also thought for some time to be closely related to the primates, but they now have their own order, Scandentia.

Common tree shrews are sexually mature at a few months old, and they mate monogamously. The male constructs two separate nests—one for the parents and one for the young. Parental care is scant; the female visits the offspring to nurse them for a few minutes every two days.

The cover image is from *Lydekker's Natural History*. The cover font is Adobe ITC Garamond. The text font is Linotype Birka; the heading font is Adobe Myriad Condensed; and the code font is LucasFont's TheSansMonoCondensed.

Have it your way.

Get even more for your money.

Join the O'Reilly Community, and register the O'Reilly books you own. It's free, and you'll get:

- $4.99 ebook upgrade offer
- 40% upgrade offer on O'Reilly print books
- Membership discounts on books and events
- Free lifetime updates to ebooks and videos
- Multiple ebook formats, DRM FREE
- Participation in the O'Reilly community
- Newsletters
- Account management
- 100% Satisfaction Guarantee

Signing up is easy:

1. Go to: oreilly.com/go/register
2. Create an O'Reilly login.
3. Provide your address.
4. Register your books.

Note: English-language books only

To order books online:
oreilly.com/store

For questions about products or an order:
orders@oreilly.com

To sign up to get topic-specific email announcements and/or news about upcoming books, conferences, special offers, and new technologies:
elists@oreilly.com

For technical questions about book content:
booktech@oreilly.com

To submit new book proposals to our editors:
proposals@oreilly.com

O'Reilly books are available in multiple DRM-free ebook formats. For more information:
oreilly.com/ebooks

O'REILLY®

Spreading the knowledge of innovators   oreilly.com

CPSIA information can be obtained at www.ICGtesting.com
Printed in the USA
BVOW031730240412

288532BV00001B/1/P